PARENTS FORUM

Where The Heart Listens

A handbook for parents and their allies
in a global society

by Eve Sullivan

DEDICATION

To parents around the world and all those who care for children and support parents.

SUPPORT

We gratefully acknowledge financial support for publication of this book from the following organizations and individuals.

Sponsors	Gravestar Foundation
Donors	Austin Grill
Contributors	Cambridge Family & Children's Service
	The Dayton Foundation
	Beverly Viemeister
	MIT Office of Government and Community Relations
	Rotary Club of Cambridge
	Angel Zamora
	Cambridge Health Alliance
Friends	Peter and Bea Britton
	Bobbie d'Alessandro
	Jolene McDaniel
	Michael Sullivan
	Joseph X. Sullivan
	Islamic Humanitarian Service
	Massé Hardware
	Somerville Lions Club
	North Cambridge Catholic H.S.
	Joanne Tashjian

and many others

i

The house represents a place where parents can meet. The open door symbolizes the welcome that PARENTS FORUM offers to all those interested in parenting and family issues, as well as the freedom that the program gives participants to come and go as their time allows and their interests determine. The window represents the program's effort to shed light on the practice of parenting, which is too often undertaken with little training or support. The sections of the fan light represent five years of program involvement, after which a participant is considered a graduate of PARENTS FORUM. The logo concept, by Eve Sullivan, was developed and realized by designer Marie Sheridan.

The circle formed by words "networking, skill development and support" represents a crystal ball in which we see our vision realized: communities where family life is celebrated and parents and others are supported in caring for children. The sides of the house represent the five areas of our lives: self care and decision making, relationships with family and friends, achievement in school and work, leisure activities, and community activities. PARENTS FORUM seeks to raise participants' awareness of the balance -- and imbalances -- in their lives among these five areas.

NOTICE

PARENTS FORUM is the trademark of our non-governmental, non-profit program. The organization's purpose is to disseminate our ideas and promote our activities. Authorization to individuals and groups to use the PARENTS FORUM trademark in association with book and toy exchanges, workshops and other events is subject to written agreement with PARENTS FORUM.

DISCLAIMER

PARENTS FORUM is not a substitute for medical, psychiatric, or psychological advice or other counseling. Readers are urged to consult their health care advisors or other appropriate professionals about specific concerns or problems.

Address inquiries to:
PARENTS FORUM
144 Pemberton Street
Cambridge, MA 02140-2509 USA

info@parentsforum.org

Library of Congress Cataloging-in-Publication
Sullivan, Eve, 1941- PARENTS FORUM
Where the Heart Listens / Eve Sullivan
ISBN   0-9703143-0-2

First Printing 2001

Design by Jana Bull
Design and Illustrations by Marie Sheridan
Illustrations by Martina Marek

Table of Contents

Dedication and Support..............................i

About our Logo..ii

Notice and Disclaimer...............................iii

CHAPTER 1
Heart of the Matter...................................... 1
CHAPTER 2
Beginnings.. 9

CHAPTER 3
From There to Here....................................21

CHAPTER 4
Tools of the Trade......................................33

CHAPTER 5
Questions not Answers..............................53

CHAPTER 6
Watch Your Words and Your Silences.......89

CHAPTER 7
Raising Parents..103

CHAPTER 8
Love and Order...119

Resources.. 125

Acknowledgments....................................191

Afterword... 197

Heart of the Matter

Chapter One

This book aspires to change the way you feel about parenting, the way you think about it, and the way you go about it. At the same time, it aspires to transform the ways we support each other as parents and the ways other individuals, agencies and businesses in our communities support us. Each task taken by itself is challenging, but there is powerful synergy among them and I am convinced that they can more easily be accomplished if we work on them at the same time.

Parenting is the oddest business: part service, as we nurture and guide our young people into adulthood, and part production, as we try to meet society's demands that our children become healthy, honest and caring, hard-working, fun-loving, and service-minded young adults. Unfortunately, most of us are pushed -- and we push ourselves -- to meet these demands with ever-shrinking resources of time or money, or both.

In a sense, our children are our clients, consumers of our parenting services. Everybody else, that is, society at large, is a client, too, expecting us to provide a satisfactory product from our home industry. But where are the parenting schools? Who provides the on-the-job training? While these analogies hardly capture the many dimensions of parenting, raising children is still a job. We need to get down to business, starting with a careful consideration of the skills we need for the job.

This book is not fundamentally about raising children, but about raising parents. We need to become the best parents we can be, and this process requires that we reach inside ourselves and that we reach out to each other. Reaching inside ourselves involves thoughtfully examining both the parenting we received and the parenting we are doing. Reaching out to each other involves talking with other parents about our successes and struggles, and theirs. These two efforts, one inward and one outward, help us to develop skills to achieve our "personal best" as parents.

We must also continue (or begin!) to advocate for the time and support we need to succeed at this most challenging and critical job. Sometimes advocacy within the family is all that's needed -- help with homemaking from one's mate or children -- but we also need to advocate outside the family. Parents' voices need to be heard and parents' needs considered in schools, at the workplace, and in government policy debate. The resources section at the end of this book describes some of the many organizations engaged in supporting parents and in bringing family issues into public debate.

In developing new skills, will we become perfect parents? Of course not. On a good day, yes, certainly we will be good parents, maybe great ones! On a not-so-good day or a truly terrible day, we can share our frustration, anger, sadness or fear with another adult rather than take those powerful feelings out on our children. We need to reach out to other parents when we are caught in our own emotional storms and when our children's storms threaten to pull us in. In doing so, we can keep the best moments we have with our kids clearly in mind and heart. These best moments come when we are emotionally present in our own lives and emotionally available to our children. We need to remember how much we love our kids, how much our kids love us and how much they need us, even when -- or especially when -- an "emotional tornado" threatens. Other parents help us do just that.

There are many books on baby care, child development, and children's learning, and countless volumes on the shelves by professionals and parents-who've-been-there about what can and does go wrong with kids and families. Still too scarce on the parenting book rack, though, is guidance for parents on specific techniques and strategies for dealing with the feelings and conflicts provoked by our own ordinary day-to-day experiences with our children. Most of us start on a positive path, with a lot of love and joy, and we want to stay on that path. But how?

A young woman who looks to me both as a friend and as "another mother" in her life (I am twenty-some years older) called me not too long ago to tell me that, after a year or more of effort, she had finally gotten a new job. She thanked me for encouraging her in the low moments. While her delight was obvious, she was emotionally "stuck" on one thing. Over and over, like a broken record she said, "I can't believe my boss (of the job she was leaving) didn't thank me." I listened, encouraged and then listened some more. My friend finally realized that it was better for her (never mind what her former boss thought) if she focused on the good wishes that other co-workers had expressed at her leaving and her own sense of

You won't find a set of rules in this book, no recommended bedtimes for a certain age child, methods for getting children to clean their rooms, or strategies to get teenagers to call you and tell you where they are. What you will find are suggestions for new ways to talk with your children and to talk with other parents about your own experiences. The suggestions will guide you in identifying your feelings and thoughts and in seeing how each affects the other and how both affect your behaviors. Often the feeling, thinking and action parts of our experiences get confused. The PARENTS FORUM approach helps you examine your feelings and thoughts before choosing what to do. You will find particular emphasis on the practice of more attentive listening and less judgmental response.

I hope this handbook will help you develop greater appreciation for what is working well in your own family. Focus on the positive aspects of family life

accomplishment. Certainly it is important and freeing to pay attention to the positive elements in our relationships and our lives. Sometimes, though, telling a friend or a parent, a sibling or spouse, over and over again how sad or angry we feel, is essential to getting to a positive place. That conversation with my young friend reminded me that we never outgrow our need for a sympathetic ear and that if parenting is about any one thing it is about fostering our children's emotional development as they grow and adapt to changing circumstances.

will give you courage and energy to consider honestly the problems you face. The discussions and exercises described in later chapters will help you develop new perspectives on what may not be working so well. The handbook also suggests sorts of activities to look for -- and to organize -- in your community where you can meet others who share your concern for healthy family life.

But parents are busy people and you may already have enough commitments! Whether you use the PARENTS FORUM approach informally, as a reference, or formally, through participation in events, I hope it will be helpful to you.

Most of us know instinctively what researchers tell us -- that human beings, as social animals, need each other in at least two different ways: We need both the intimacy that comes from close relationships and the affiliation that comes from belonging to a group. Without these connections, we feel lonely and isolated. Participating in PARENTS FORUM gives people a chance to make new friends and practice communications skills that can help us strengthen our relationships with family members. At the same time, PARENTS FORUM activities connect participants to their communities, fulfilling the need for group affiliation.

You may have picked up this book because you are concerned about stress or unhappiness you have noticed in yourself or a friend or family member. Maybe someone gave you this book because he or she is concerned about you or your children. Perhaps you have young children -- or no children yet -- and you want to look down the road ahead to see what sharp turns and scenic overlooks await you on the parenting journey. However this book got to you, I am glad you have it in hand.

Perhaps you could say PARENTS FORUM is a program of "smart love," in that we seek to create a better balance between discipline and affection in our family lives. In sharing our stories -- describing the events of our lives, our reactions and those of people around us, and the eventual outcomes -- we raise our social and emotional intelligence quotient. We become more effective and more loving parents as, using the skills we acquire in PARENTS FORUM, we learn to listen with our hearts.

Beginnings

Chapter Two

PARENTS FORUM grew out of a serious family crisis. Some years ago, one of my teenage children started getting into trouble both in and out of school and began drinking and using other drugs. Within a year, his behavior was out of control. Despite the efforts of teachers, doctors, counselors, and court officers who all tried to help us, his father and I did not find effective, long-term support for our son or ourselves in any traditional setting. My husband and I had separated not long before our son's problems began and we later divorced. In looking back, I don't believe that my son's misbehavior caused the divorce or that the divorce caused his misbehavior -- although certainly each made the other more difficult to handle. I do think, however, that the roots of both may be traced to difficulties we all had in communicating our feelings.

In our early search for help, the focus was always on my son but, in fact, I was as troubled as he was and didn't realize it. My fear and anger, my "control-o-mania," got in the way of everything! Successful resolution of our shared problems eventually came when we participated in a therapeutic community focused on recovery from addiction, particularly alcohol and other drug abuse. The program, which my ex-husband found for us through a friend, succeeded in helping us all make positive changes. I often wonder now whether improving our communications skills earlier would have helped us avoid many of the conflicts we experienced. At the very least, better communication skills would have helped us manage those conflicts more effectively and treat each other more respectfully. We found the help our family needed through Straight New England, a day-treatment program for young people with substance abuse problems. Founded in the mid-1980s, Straight was a controversial program that has since disbanded. Its unique residential component placed new clients in the homes of families of other young people who had been in the program several months or more. Parents received support for their own recovery (from "co-alcoholism" or codependency) as well as training in how to guide their own child and their "host son" or "host daughter" on the path to recovery.

Professional addictions recovery staff directed the daily treatment, interviewed parents, and monitored the "host homes" to assure compliance with state safety regulations. Funded in part by families' medical insurance, through fees assessed to parents, and by fundraising undertaken by parents, the program had its critics -- and it certainly did not work for everyone. But when it worked, as it did in our case, it seemed to work miracles. The angry, self-destructive teenager we brought to Straight became, over the course of twenty months, a confident and purposeful young man.

As clients in Straight for almost two years, our troubled son, his brothers, his father and I, along with several hundred other families, learned how substance abuse affects both individuals and families. In Straight we learned that alcoholism, or any addiction, is basically a disease of the feelings. With a lot of hard work, my ex-husband and I each succeeded in rebuilding our relationship with our son. This rebuilding was preceded by some "un-building," as we examined our past experiences to discover the interlocking, unhealthy roles we each played under the influence of substance abuse. To accomplish this, we were charged with two main tasks. First, we had to learn to be emotionally honest, that is, to allow ourselves to experience our feelings and, as appropriate, to express feelings, thoughts, and

11

desires in words without blaming ourselves or others. Second, we had to learn to expect and encourage others to do the same.

Since that desperate time, now happily over, I have seen how putting the lessons of recovery to work in day-to-day family situations can dramatically alter one's perspective even if it does not always alter the outcome of the situation. I've found that the usefulness of these lessons extends to situations involving difficult people and challenges at work and elsewhere outside family life.

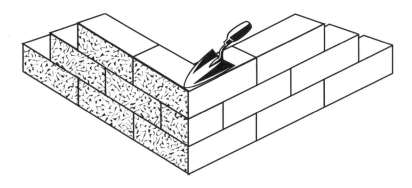

In the Straight parent network, none of us worried about the differences of race, religion, class or social standing that can loom large in ordinary life. We focused instead on the collective safety and individual recovery of our young people and, with those shared concerns foremost in our minds, we helped each other out. In their daily group meetings, our teenagers talked about past injuries they had suffered -- and injuries they had inflicted -- in their families, and they confronted each other about following the steps to recovery and the rules of the program. In twice weekly parent meetings, we adults did the same.

A central element in our parent meetings involved reevaluating a past incident we recalled -- for example, a night when a teen came home drunk, or didn't come home at all, or a time when the police called after stopping a young person for reckless driving -- and describing our feelings about the incident without accusing or shaming the young person. Limiting the discussion to one specific incident was essential, as it kept us from launching into a series of accusations ("And another thing...!") and kept both parent and young person "on the same page." Through this exercise, we parents helped each other learn to separate our feelings from our thoughts and to express both without labeling our teenagers. We also learned to separate our feelings about our kids -- love, admiration, hope -- from our feelings about their misbehaviors -- disappointment, disapproval, desperation.

Over time, we learned how to have honest and, at the same time, sensitive conversations about our differences, how to be both clear and respectful in discussing difficult issues. In my family, these conversations, at first awkward, were a refreshing change from the yelling, name-calling and swearing, and from the troubled, punishing silences that marked the time when my son was actively using alcohol and other drugs.

These conversations were different, too, from the negative view of family life too often portrayed in television situation comedies, where insult is humor and put-downs are frequently viewed as victories. In fact, to reduce this negative influence, television viewing for Straight families was restricted to a single approved video or a special broadcast on Sundays. Listening to the radio or to recorded music was also restricted, since the program's philosophy held that the messages contained in news shows and popular music undermined the recovery work that was our focus.

Straight clients and their families progressed through five phases before completing the program. First-phase clients, called "newcomers," were required to focus on themselves as individuals. In second phase, we focused on relationships with family and friends. In third phase the recovering young people went back to school or to work. In fourth phase they were given days off, taking responsibility for planning outings and activities free from alcohol and other drugs. Finally, in fifth phase, both young people and parents were given the privilege of standing at the side of group, in positions of authority, at our community meetings.

We drove seemingly endless miles to attend Monday and Friday night parent meetings and to take recovering young people to meet the van fer-  *rying them six days a week to the treatment center outside Boston. Sharing lukewarm potluck dinners, we gathered in the carpeted reception area of a large warehouse building, to socialize before the recovery-focused meetings. These always lasted too long, testing our commitment, I guess! In and out of meetings, we cried and laughed and sang. Day by day, helping each other, we got better.*

If a client in a higher phase ran from the program, the progression was interrupted. After returning or being brought back from "cop-outs," clients had to repeat the five-phase sequence starting with Phase One. This practice reinforced the importance of focusing on oneself and served a valuable purpose: holding teens and parents each accountable for their own individual recovery.

Long before I found myself involved in recovery with my family, when I began raising my boys years ago, I knew I wanted to be different from my own parents. But I didn't know how to make changes or even where to look for models. Although they loved me, my parents misused their strength and power. They doubtless had few models for effective conflict resolution and, as a result, their disagreements sometimes led to shouting, or worse, to breaking each others' possessions. Both the disagreements and the destruction terrified me. The fear I sometimes felt made me treasure all the more dearly the many happy times -- exploring the woods, raising chickens and goats, celebrating birthdays, and doing ordinary art projects, crafts and gardening -- that formed the positive foundation of our family life. Unfortunately, while it may be true that the positive experiences took up more time in my childhood, it is my parents' rageful outbursts that occupy center stage in my childhood memories.

As a mother of young children, I repeated many of the creative activities that were so memorable for me as a child. At the same time, I found myself engaging in conflicts with my husband and my sons that were painfully similar to those I remembered from my own growing-up. While I struggled to provide adequate measures of love and positive discipline for my sons, minor conflicts, over

15

dinnertime or baths, chores or television, easily became major ones.

When the boys were little, I could not see my part in these conflicts. In my son's recovery program, however, I learned how the tone of voice and choice of words in my response -- and whether I responded or not -- could help or hinder a peaceful resolution of conflict. As I learned to let go of the "control-o-mania" that was my addiction, I gave my son room to recover from his alcohol and other drug dependency. I became more solution-oriented as a parent and as a person.

Now that the crisis of my son's teenage years has passed, I can look back and see how other parents, both within the Straight community and beyond, helped me in my efforts to make positive changes and how, in our friendships, we refined our communications skills and created some new models for parenting. Day-to-day, my friends listen to me, sympathize with me, and encourage me. And so do my children, now. They also give me honest criticism, if I ask them.

A few years back, a co-worker related a story that gave me a painful flashback to my own now-distant crazy days. He had been riding the subway to work and saw a woman and a playful seven-year-old boy in tow, probably her son. She said to the boy, "I'm gonna slap you... and I'm going to enjoy it. Keep it up, wiseass. I don't find you amusing at all." My coworker was shocked and wrote the woman's words down to give me, knowing I worked with parents. What can you say when you hear a stranger say something like that? Could you say gently, "It's

Letting go of my need to manage things that are not mine to manage has been an uneven and difficult process, with both intellectual and emotional elements. I may know in my head that one of my boys doesn't need help with a challenge he faces, but in my heart I want to do something for him. The reverse may also be true: I might be quite at ease not offering any assistance but have a nagging thought that I should say or do something to help, and I have to depend on my sons, who are now young adults, to tell me if this is so. Since our children's needs change frequently throughout their early years and into adulthood as well, it can be a challenge to strike the right balance: to do enough, but not too much.

But on a daily basis, I have to realize and accept

*rough getting out early like this. He'll be fine."
Most of us, out of the hurt or fear or embarrassment
that underlies anger, at one time or another use
words we regret in speaking to our children. Don't
you imagine that the woman on the subway was
raised in a climate of verbal abuse and probably
physical abuse as well? From other parents and in
parent education programs, I have learned ways of
handling my own emotional travel so that, for the
most part, I can steer clear of such destructive confrontations as the one just described.*

that my children's lives are their own, separate and independent from mine. And ultimately, this perspective has improved my ability to listen to them. I can usually hear what they have to say without recalling or re-experiencing the anger, fear and sadness that colored so much of the past. If strong feelings do come up for me in a conversation or an argument with one of my children, I know enough to call a friend and ask for support, perspective, and advice.

By talking with other parents and asking yourself hard questions about your motivations, you can see your family situation more clearly. Even if you find yourself veering off the happy and loving path you first envisioned for yourself and your family, you will be able to identify problems when they are still manageable. You may also be better able to seek the advice and support of family and friends, or professional help if necessary, before a situation becomes critical.

More than once, my youngest son said to me when I was on the verge of losing either my composure or my temper, "Mom,  *you need to call Bonny." Bonny is a long-time good friend who has A-number-one listening skills! My son has learned that if someone listens to his mother for a bit, she will be better able to listen to him. Perhaps a young person's endorsement is the best consumer report for the practice of parents listening to each other!*

I have seen myself and my children make small, consistent changes in the way we communicate with each other. Since they are young adults (turning 20, 28 and 30 the year I write this), my sons don't need the kind of mothering I so enjoyed giving in the past. In a way, we are both farther apart and closer now. The space allows the intimacy first to happen and then to grow. I no longer pretend, or even aspire, to be a "supermom." Instead, I am content that we speak to each other often. We share worries, joys, plans and sometimes just listen to each other. On occasion, I find I need to apologize for something I've said or done and they do the same. What do you know... we're human!

Other parents have helped me. I hope this book helps you to ask for and get what you need from other parents. We can help each other.

From There to Here
Chapter Three

It became clear, about half way through my son's treatment, that the habits of emotional honesty learned in recovery were helpful to me as a person and as a parent in many ways entirely unrelated to alcohol and other drug abuse. It also became clear to me that these lessons could be useful to people who did not have any experience of addictions in their families. Why not a positive program for parents who simply want to improve their family lives?

As a former teacher of English and French, I realized that much of what I had learned was, in a sense, a new language. If I could learn it, I could teach it. Further, I saw that the lessons of recovery could be incorporated into a program that parents

Aa Bb Cc Dd Ee

in any community could run for themselves. So I started writing the lessons down. Then I started a column in the neighborhood paper, *The North Cambridge News*, in Cambridge, Massachusetts, where I live.

Enlisting the help of friends and a college volunteer, I began organizing activities. The first event was a poster workshop for children held at a local library. Entitled "What do you like about your family?" the workshop attracted a few individual parents and kids, a group of children from an after-school program with their teachers, and a reporter from a local TV station. The energy we all felt that day -- and the media attention we received -- kept us moving forward. Next, we organized a book and toy exchange, again at the library. Soon after these initial successes, we developed workshops and found a school willing to host them. We did a "trial run" of our format, which was based on eight fundamental questions designed to evaluate our parenting skills and deficits.

Many sympathetic community members and leaders, librarians especially, encouraged and helped us in these efforts. In addition, I attended every parenting workshop and conference I could get to locally as well as several in other cities and a few in other countries. One good friend, another, and then another, agreed to help us incorporate and seek non-profit status.

What should we call the program? "Positive-program-for-ordinary-parents-with-garden-variety-kids-and-day-to-day-run-of-the-mill-challenges" was good, but too long for a banner. After a careful search and much deliberation, we chose the name PARENTS FORUM. At the start, we proposed two themes for our activities: parent support and family celebration. In our third year, we clarified our vision, mission, and goals, settling finally on three themes: networking, skill development and support. Some time after that, we added the tag line "where the heart listens" to emphasize that listening, especially listening to expressions of emotion, is central to our program.

While PARENTS FORUM takes inspiration from the recovery movement, it also draws on my experiences as a "room parent" for over twelve years at my sons' grammar school, on nearly 20 years of hosting international visitors in my home and on my teaching abroad -- a year in Tunisia and a year in Portugal. In addition, my youngest son's interest in American Sign Language opened the doors for me to the Deaf community, whose members have a special bond defined by their gestural language. They also face special challenges in family communication, I realized, as nine out of ten Deaf children are born to hearing parents.

At an early PARENTS FORUM meeting, a young mother decided the group was not right for her because no one else had a two-year-old. Certainly parents of older children could have given her some new perspectives on the misnamed "terrible twos" which can, in fact, be terrific! If my kids are boys, mostly grown, and yours are infant girls or pre-schoolers, does that mean we have nothing to say to one another on the topic of family life? Of course not! Exploring our differences and finding common ground benefits all of us, whether we are interacting parent-to-parent within a shared culture or across

In addition, I have been fortunate to have access to a variety of seminars offered at the university where I work. The advice and expertise of trained professionals on topics ranging from forming playgroups to financial planning has influenced me personally and has, in turn, influenced PARENTS FORUM. In fact, perhaps surprisingly, some very useful perspectives on parenting have come from staff development courses I have attended at work.

While our children are not our employees nor are we, strictly speaking, our children's "bosses," our kids and our households definitely need managing. Management training can offer valuable insights on the dynamics of supervising and motivating others. What four-year-old doesn't need supervising? What eight-year-old doesn't need motivating? Even customer service manuals offer useful guidance. There will be times when the customer (your twelve-year-old?) cannot get the product or service he wants (movie money? a ride into town or to the mall?) and you, as "parenting service provider" have to say "No"

cultures. Besides the individual differences that may get in the way of our supporting each other -- age, gender, personality, education -- there are larger differences, such as race, religion, language, culture, and class. It does little good to ignore the differences. The best we can do is recognize and honor them. And try to look beyond.

clearly and effectively while retaining the "customer's" goodwill. All right, maybe that's stretching
the metaphor, but I hope you see my point.

Still, as informative and helpful as professionally led
seminars can be, they cannot replace the warm,
personal support shared among parents -- for free!
-- when we get together to talk. PARENTS FORUM
claims a section of middle ground between informal
waiting-for-the-school-bell conversations among
parents and informative (but sometimes intimidat-
ing) presentations by professionals on child development and parenting strategies. We certainly don't
want to replace either one, but strive to incorporate
good elements from both. In any case, we offer an
opportunity for unhurried and non-judgmental parent-to-parent conversations.

When I meet someone new at work or in a social
setting and the conversation turns to family life, as
it often does, I am struck by two things: the depth
of our shared concern for the well-being of our family members -- children, siblings, parents -- and the
many differences that stand in the way of our sharing that concern.

Because our concerns, and our conversations, often
focus on problems we face, it is easy to lose sight of
the fact that kids are fun! Raising children is difficult, but it can also be the most joyful and reward-
ing part of our lives. It is surely the most important.
When we are stuck in a bedtime battle with a four-
year-old or tearing our hair out over a fourteen-
year-old missing curfew, we may forget the joy of
seeing our children take their first steps, of hearing
them babble their first words (or seeing Deaf children's early sign-babble). But if we can keep the
good times in mind, we have a better chance of

overcoming both the difficulties we face and the differences that divide us.

Difficult situations, from simple to nearly insurmountable, arise in every family, as do differences of opinion. This basic, inescapable fact of family life inspired a core element of PARENTS FORUM: helping parents focus on the way they handle conflict. Regardless of our backgrounds, when and how we approach and/or avoid conflict reveals our true values to our children. As they move out into the world -- in playgroups, at neighborhood parks, in school and eventually at work -- they take their cues from us on conflict resolution.

As any parent knows, raising kids is much more than a walk in the park or a day at the beach, although these tranquil moments are absolutely essential and keep us going in the less-than-peaceful times. For better or for worse, raising children also involves the "screaming meemies" and the fall-out from declarations such as "I will not wear those shoes!" ... "I told you to be home on time for dinner!" ... "I'm quitting school!" and "I hate you!" These confrontations test our parental mettle. In PARENTS FORUM workshops, we help each other look at the examples we are setting as we navigate and negotiate our way through these day-to-day hassles.

Parenting styles can range from authoritarian to permissive, from dictator to doormat. Of course neither extreme is effective in all situations or over the long term. We incorporated into our program a model (described in Mary Pipher's book *Reviving Ophelia* and used in other parent programs too) for evaluating our parenting style that helped us find ways to be authoritative without being dictatorial, and ways

I have often found that a struggle (getting a child to bed on time) or argument (getting help with housework) gives me an admittedly unhealthy satisfaction. Thoughts like "Poor me ...the kids give me no peace. ...I do all the work. ...they are ungrateful wretches" keep me from seeing the good in my kid and in me and -- just as important -- keep me from changing the way I approach a struggle. That unhealthy desire for self-satisfaction comes, I think, when I want to be in control -- to impose my will on my child -- more than I want to have a productive, if heated, conversation with my child. The win-win approach to parenting can work, but only when I give up the "kick" of control, without giving up parental responsibility. Then I am able to set clear standards and have my children follow the rules ....well, most of the time.

to be loving without letting our kids walk all over us.
At the heart of parenting, of course, in times of conflict or contentment, is communication. As we developed PARENTS FORUM workshops, we adapted
a few tools from the Straight treatment program
that had proven invaluable in helping my family
resolve our communication problems. These include
an examination of the balance in our lives (the
handy guide), an exercise for identifying our feelings
(feelings list) and a conversational formula for talking about our feelings. With these tools, the Straight
program had helped me to create a new base of
emotional and intellectual honesty, right under-
neath my feet. On this firmer ground, I found the
courage to ask myself some questions I had not
thought of before. As these questions evolved, the
teacher in me wanted to share what I had learned.
A simple curriculum based on eight questions
evolved, designed to teach others what I had learned
through such desperation.

One essential theme running through all eight questions, taking a purely personal view, is, "What is the
role of this activity, challenge or conflict in my life?"
The other essential theme, taking an interpersonal
view, is "Do I need help -- or do you need my help --
with this?" As a mother I started out doing, or
arranging, or managing everything for my kids. I
thought that was my job. But as a child grows, the
job changes. If I hold on too tight or do too much,
my son or daughter has too little opportunity to
learn and grow. In fact, many of the struggles that
come up in conversations and in our workshops
have to do with judging when to hold on and when
to let go. Simple role-plays accompany several of the
questions. These dramatic (and sometimes melodra-
matic) interludes help us look at our behaviors,
especially on occasions of our children's misbehav-

ior. With these role-plays and the discussions that follow them, we are able to uncover the issues motivating and the concerns fueling the conflicts we experience. In the process we often discover strategies for handling the conflicts in a positive way.

We believe that putting the PARENTS FORUM workshop tools and questions to use in everyday interactions with family and friends could help parents discover -- or develop -- and follow the rules they need to be the best they can be, on any given day. Whether in private reflection, conversation with spouse, partner or friend, or in group discussion, the tools and questions enable individuals to clarify the issues that concern them, the challenges they face, and the choices they have.

The idea for PARENTS FORUM was clear: a positive program for parents. But how could we get parents who did not have any pressing problems to get together and talk about what was going right in their lives? We knew we needed to offer parents incentives or rewards of some sort, like the lollipops (now story books) that doctors give along with immunizations. So we came up with the idea of having a prize drawing at each of our workshops and other events.

In our early PARENTS FORUM efforts to get donations of prizes (restaurant and book or toy store gift certificates, movie and museum passes) for parents, we found local merchants intrigued by our idea of a positive program and generally supportive. Some board members have joked that "No one has ever said 'no' to us" -- and it's almost true. Most people really want to support children and families in their communities and welcome opportunities to do so. These solicitations accomplish two goals besides meeting program costs: they get parents talking (sometimes even bragging) about how they are helping each other and becoming better parents and, at the same time, they let other people in the community know about and share in those efforts.

We had a small group of people committed to building PARENTS FORUM as an organization and, supporting this core group, a network of friends and community people interested in helping the program succeed. Support from the business commu-

nity along with recognition and donations from service clubs -- Rotary, Lions, Kiwanis -- have been key to our success.

From simple beginnings, PARENTS FORUM has taken shape. We continue to run book and toy exchanges in Cambridge and Somerville, Massachusetts, about two a year. We have tables at local fairs and parent-teacher nights at schools. As our time, energy and funds allowed, we take part in conferences given by organizations with similar goals. Whenever possible, we offer PARENTS FORUM workshops for parent groups, usually at schools. We are taking our place in a much larger community of individuals and other organizations committed to supporting families.

Tools of the Trade
Chapter Four

The tools of the PARENTS FORUM program help us "tune up" our parenting skills. If you like the image of a car rolling smoothly along life's highway, think of the process as mechanical. If you envision your family singing in harmony, think of it as musical. Someone has to drive the car or direct the choir and it's us: parents. We have to be the responsible ones, even on days when we don't feel able to manage the household or mind the children, and even when our children insist that they don't need us. We use our "tools of the trade" in exercises that focus, not on our kids, but on ourselves.

This chapter describes in detail the three basic tools we have devised: the handy guide, feelings list, and conversational formula, mentioned briefly in the previous chapter. Exercises accompany each tool and you can work through these alone or with another parent. Designed in part to help you consider your personal strengths and weaknesses, they will also help you identify behaviors -- both your own and those of family members -- that you would like to target for change.

With the first tool, a handy guide, you consider the balance or lack of balance -- and the sometimes competing demands -- of five areas of your life. These are (1) self-care and decision-making, (2) relationships with family and friends, (3) achievement in school or work, (4) leisure activities, and (5) community activities. To create this guide, put one hand down on a blank sheet of paper with your fingers spread apart. With a pencil in the other hand, trace your hand shape - just as you probably did as a kid. Then label your thumb, 1 - self-care, and the other fingers, in order, 2 - relationships, 3 - achievement, 4 - leisure, and 5 - community.

In a PARENTS FORUM workshop we begin with this handy guide. Ordinary life rarely allows us time to focus on the balance among these five kinds of

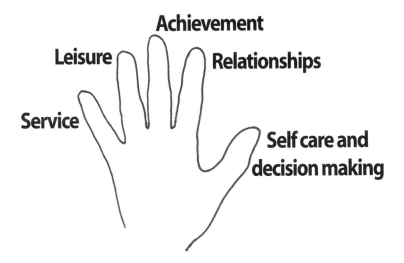

Achievement

Leisure

Relationships

Service

Self care and decision making

activities -- we are usually too busy engaged in one activity or another. You can do this on your own. Take the guide you have drawn and note beside each finger something you have done in that category in the last week. You may find it difficult to decide which activity to put where, since an activity can fit into more than one category. For example, you can play soccer for exercise (self-care), as a way to enjoy the company of family or friends (relationships), as a paid coach or player (achievement), as something you do for fun (leisure), or as a volunteer coach in a youth league (service).

Taking another example, you may be paid to do housework if you work as a cook or cleaning person. Most of us who are raising children, though, do food shopping, cooking, cleaning and laundry without pay. Are these tasks less achievement, then, and more service? They are both, of course, and ought to be recognized as such within the family and in the community!

Almost anything you do -- gardening, cooking, carpentry, sewing, painting, fixing cars, caring for animals, cleaning, driving -- the practice of any skill or talent, can fulfill any one of the five areas. What you

> *As a new mother, at home with my first child, I sometimes felt terribly lonely, missing the companionship of students and other teachers. I felt jobless! I was working harder than ever but without the status of a place to work and a paycheck. I often wondered if I should get a uniform. Should there be homemaker badges, to be worn proudly by women and, now, also men who are stay-at-home parents? Recently I have seen designated parking spaces in some lots marked for "Parents with Young Children." Good idea! Official recognition could go a long way toward countering the ridiculous idea that parents at home with children do not work. We can begin by saying of people who are parenting full-time, "They do not work outside the home."*

consider play may seem like work to me. My paid work may be the same as someone else's volunteer service. As you complete this exercise, noting an activity for each part of the handy guide, even if it is difficult to fit an activity in only one category, take a moment to reflect on the week gone by. How did you feel while you were involved in each activity? How do you feel now that it is done?

Consider whether the time you spent and the satisfaction you gained in each activity is what you would like it to be. Would you like to spend more time alone or on activities of your own choosing?

One workshop participant told a story of her five-year-old daughter coming home from kindergarten with a picture of the whole family, and there was mom, with five arms and hands. Puzzled, she asked her little girl, "Why does Mommy have all those hands?" The answer came back, "You're always so busy." She found a lesson there. Maybe, she realized, I don't need to spend so much energy and time doing things. Maybe I need to spend a little more time just being with my kid.

...with family members or friends? ...at work? ...having fun? ...in community activities? Remember that the exercise is only for assessment, not judgment. Set aside the "shoulds" and look at what you actually do. Consider what you would like to do more of, or less of, without worrying about whether a change is possible. Limiting the evaluation to one week makes it easier to be honest and specific about imbalances in our lives that the handy guide may reveal.

Setting aside the handy guide, we move on to our second tool, a feelings list. Creating this list can be harder than it seems, as our minds may wander off into what we think, or what we think we should feel, or how someone else told us we should, or shouldn't, feel. Take the handy guide you made and write a feeling next to each activity. For example, "I felt refreshed after my walk to the train station," "I felt annoyed about the expense of getting the car repaired," "I felt grateful for my health after visiting my sick relative in the hospital," "I felt resentful about putting in extra time on the school volunteer project."

Starting with the feelings that you listed for the activities you described, try filling a whole sheet with feeling words. Your list, if it's something like mine, may have started off with happy, sad, afraid, angry (the basic four) and moved on to confused (a convenient catchall if you can't come up with a specific feeling word), or perhaps frustrated, amused, relieved, lonely, and so on. Often physical sensations -- tired, thirsty, sore -- are easier to name than feelings, but try to find words for emotions, as many as you can. It may be enough to make the list once and keep it somewhere convenient, in your wallet or handbag or on the refrigerator, but you can also add to it from time to time.

Making this list may seem like a tedious exercise, but it is actually very important. Because demands of daily life are often pressing -- our thoughts may come in a rush and events often require immediate action -- it can be enormously helpful to take the time and make a special effort to become aware of our emotions.

When our family started the Straight treatment program, we were given a feelings list. At the outset, I saw it only as words on a page and had no idea of the key role it would play in my own -- and my son's -- recovery. But my determination to do whatever it took to help him propelled me through the discomfort of examining my feelings. As instructed, I kept the list with me -- like vocabulary words in a new language -- looked at it frequently, adding notes and new words. I'd refer to it especially when I got angry or when someone got angry with me, as we were told that anger is often a mask for other feelings. I began to see the list's value in helping me get to the root of my emotional turmoil. When someone (a child, coworker or boss) interrupts me in the middle of a task, I may first feel angry at the person but then realize that I feel confused by the interruption. If I can tell the person that, or simply take a moment to catch my breath and "shift gears," I am able to respond more calmly.

Anger is a fact of life, sometimes justified and often helpful (for example, in warding off threats), but it is seldom simple. With the feelings list in hand, or at least in mind, I learned to respond rather than react

In more than one telephone conversation with my ex-husband, I felt angry enough (about money or custody or whatever) to slam the receiver down. He probably felt the same way. Keeping in mind the idea of anger-as-a-mask, I could see that behind my anger was resentment about losing time with my children -- his children, too, of course -- or fear about not having enough money to pay for the things or the activities I thought the boys should have. With that perspective on my own mixed feelings, I realized he had some of the same mixed feelings. This insight helped me to be less defensive and, usually, negotiate more reasonably with him.

to my own feelings of anger and to angry outbursts in other people, including my children. I shared the list with many friends and, in developing PARENTS FORUM, realized that it had to be a key element in our program.

Of course anger is not the only strong feeling. Fear and grief can overwhelm us, as can more positive feelings. People do, after all, sometimes weep for joy! Somehow, probably from my parents, I got the notion that being a grownup meant being in charge of myself and "in control" of my feelings. This, in fact, is only half true. While I need to learn to take charge of my life -- think things through and act responsibly -- my feelings are what they are. I now realize that I spent a lot of my childhood (and my adulthood!) resisting them.

Recovery compelled me to break down the internal emotional dam I had built up. Dismantling that dam involved two related tasks. First, I needed to let myself experience my emotions, a physical process. I did a good bit of crying -- and laughing -- in Straight, as did just about everyone else, teens and parents alike. Second, I needed to learn to acknowledge how I felt -- at times angry, fearful, resentful, relieved -- recognize and name these feelings, a mental process. Ironically, in my efforts to be a good mother, I had tried to teach my children to do this, yet I seldom did so myself. We adults are generally expected to "keep it together" but we lose something important in the process. In learning to disguise our feelings, often for valid social reasons, we lose contact with a wellspring of energy within us.

Whether we're laughing, crying, ranting or raving, we can encourage and support each other. Our discussions in PARENTS FORUM sometimes bring up powerful feelings! Our love for our kids is so strong that it should be no surprise that the fear, sadness and anger we sometimes experience in dealing with them are equally strong.

Anger is natural, normal and important. It helps us set boundaries and right wrongs. But when anger takes the place of a full range of emotional expression -- as it too often can for men and boys -- either it becomes a shield for other natural, normal and important feelings or, worse, it can become a weapon.

I remember my father as a funny and affectionate man. When I was small he used to make up stories with me as the lead character and my teddy bear "Moanie" -- short for "Pandemonium" -- in a supporting role, along with the chickens that he and my mother raised in the backyard of the small town in Ohio where we lived. I remember waiting eagerly for the next episode of "Moanie and Chickie and Me." There were times, though, when the funny and caring dad I knew and loved "lost it" and his anger got the better of him. Those memories are equally strongly etched in my memory.

 One of the scariest moments of my childhood occurred when I was about seven or eight years old and accidentally knocked a treasured piece of sculpture off a low table in our living room. One of a pair of ivory elephant bookends, it got chipped when it hit the floor. My father, furious that I had ruined something special to him -- even though I had not done it on purpose -- took the other, undamaged ivory elephant and smashed it to pieces on the floor. Although he

didn't hit me, I felt terrified at his rage. I felt over-whelmed with regret that I had broken something beautiful that he cared so much about. I must have felt worse that I brought him to such fury, but my overwhelming recollection is one of numbness and cold fear.

When I remember the incident I always imagine myself much younger than I was at the time, proba-bly because I felt so small! I certainly don't recall our talking about what happened nor do I remem-ber my father giving me a chance to apologize or make amends. All that remains is the image of him holding the ivory elephant up over his head. And me terrified, not even able to cry. With the benefit of hindsight -- and as a parent I "lost it" more than a few times with my own children -- I can see how my father could have handled the situation differently. Perhaps, if my dad had been in a group like PAR-ENTS FORUM, he might have learned how damag-ing an uncontrolled expression of a parent's anger is to a child. He might have known how threatening it is to destroy possessions violently. He might have realized the intensity of his anger and chosen a dif-ferent way to express it. Perhaps he could even have cried. He might have given me a chance to cry and express my regret and my desire to make it up to him. Perhaps the piece I had broken off the bookend could have been glued back on. Certainly the dam-age to our relationship caused by such a rageful outburst would have been avoided.

Remembering the fear I experienced then, and feel-ing it again, yes, often shaking and crying as I retell the story, gives me energy to write this book. I hope my telling it will impress on parents how important it is for us to moderate our responses when our kids do what they do. Try thinking back to times when you have "lost it" with your kids and then further back to see if these experiences remind you of others in your own childhood. It is so common for us to inadvertently repeat our parents' mistakes despite our firm intention not to! When we recognize the roots of current struggles we are more likely to avoid injuring our kids in ways we may have been injured in the past.

Kids break things, come home late, and mess up the house, but so do grownups. On more than one occasion I have recognized a fury in my own heart similar to my dad's when I broke that ivory elephant. Now I work hard to remember to catch my breath

and let myself shake or cry or perspire -- and count to ten -- then use words and choose them carefully, avoiding hateful, abusive, or shaming language. As a less than perfect parent, I don't always succeed, but I have brought my average up considerably.

We are born having feelings -- a grabby one-year-old, a defiant two-year-old and rebellious teens remind us if we forget -- and we have to learn to be aware of our own and others' feelings. While a vital element of our job as parents is to teach our kids to monitor and manage their feelings, we are more effective at this task if we continually develop our own emotional awareness, if we "model the behavior."

Until tuning in to feelings is something you do comfortably, it is really helpful to make time for this exercise with another adult, or with one of your children, on a regular basis, perhaps once a week, and even better, once a day. The end of the day, as part of bedtime routine, before reading a story, might be a moment to weave feeling themes into conversation with your children. Take turns, timed if you like, talking with your kids about how you feel. Individual reflection is helpful too. Mornings, if you get up before your children, or evenings after they are asleep, may be good times to do some journal writing on feelings. At the very least, keep adding to your feelings list. The goals of the exercises are to become more aware of what you are feeling and to become better at expressing how you feel, out loud, to someone else.

In our first PARENTS FORUM workshops, we often found it difficult to get parents to focus on themselves. They would initially object to the exercises on the grounds that they should be talking about their children. After a while, though, by explicitly honoring listening and without insisting that people talk, we usually found participants entered into lively discussion of the past week's activities and their feelings about them. At the end of the workshops, when we asked for feedback, people almost always commented on how refreshing it was to take time to focus on their own feelings. One mother told us, "The workshop discussions held up a mirror for us to look at our family life rather than require us to talk about family issues. They were very helpful and challenging."

The handy guide and feelings list prepare the way for the third basic PARENTS FORUM tool: a conversational formula. The first few times, or the first dozen times, you use this formula, it will probably feel strange because it is different from common ways we express ourselves. In the midst of conflict, people often say things like "You make me mad!" "Stop bothering me!" "Shut (expletive deleted) up!" The conversational formula requires that you name the feeling you have, describe the specific behavior prompting the feeling, and then state the thought (or idea, or principle) that explains the situation. It goes like this:

I feel ___ (a word from your list) about ___ (an event or behavior) because ___ (a principle or a rule).

At first the formula can feel artificial, perhaps because we so easily confuse feelings with thoughts, or because we learned that some feelings are considered "bad" and are better not revealed. Practice with the conversational formula is best done when you are not under immediate stress, but the tool is especially useful when feelings run high. A doctor takes a patient's temperature and blood pressure at routine check-ups in order to get baseline measurements. So too, if we become aware of our emotions in ordinary, calm times, we have a reference point for times when we are stressed.

Here are some examples:

"I feel frustrated about missing my daily exercise because it is important for my health." "I feel confident about my son's return to school this fall because he has a good friend in his homeroom who is doing well academically." "I feel confused about visiting my homeplace because a family member seems angry with me."

Of course, the same situation can generate more than one feeling: "I feel relieved about my boss coming back from travel because I'll be able to ask him questions about work" and "I feel anxious about his return because if I make mistakes he will see them right away."

It is easy to confuse thoughts with feelings. Sometimes the phrase "I feel that...," slips into our speech, usually followed by a thought, for example, "I feel that, to be fair, you should cook dinner tonight." If you give yourself a little more time, you might be able to say, "I feel resentful at having to make dinner again tonight because we agreed to share the cooking." Having said that, and even if your partner hasn't responded, you might be able to frame a request using a feeling word, "I would feel really grateful if you make dinner tonight." Notice ...no name-calling (You're a stinker!) ....no wild accusations (You never do anything in the kitchen!) ...no self-pity (When's the last time you even picked up a dirty dish -- I have to do everything!). These histrionics do nothing to get dinner on the table or to enhance family relationships.

Also beware of using a word like "convinced" where a feeling word could go. You might think to yourself, "I feel convinced that my daughter is spending too much time with her boyfriend and not enough on her studies." Talking with your daughter directly, you might set aside your firm conviction (although you do know what's right) and say, "I feel worried about your spending a lot of time with your boyfriend because you are neglecting your school work." She might or might not share your concern for academic success, but you have been honest with your worry. She might realize that she's a little worried too, although she might not tell you right away.

Modify these examples to suit yourself: "I feel pleased about taking a long walk last Sunday because it was enjoyable and afterwards I slept well." "I feel relieved about having a telephone visit with my sister because we are each under a lot of stress and our conversation gave us both a nice lift." "I feel resentful about spending Saturday cleaning the garage because my wife/husband/kids didn't help." and, perhaps, "I feel accomplished about cleaning the garage by myself because it was a big job."

Would you ever be able to say, "I feel appreciated for cleaning the garage because my family thanked me, made dinner and did the dishes"? Doubtful. But realizing that you want appreciation is a step toward asking for it.

Making a conscious effort to consider your own feelings is good for you in a number of ways. In the short term it may keep you from "flying off the handle" when you are angry. It can help you empathize with your children or spouse in their anger, sadness or fear. Taking a longer view, this effort to raise your emotional consciousness can help you better organize your daily life. Look back at the handy guide you made. Remember that you were asked to consider what you would like to do more of, or less of, without worrying about whether a change is possible.

Now think about whether changes are possible and what changes you would like to make. Remember that "the journey of a thousand miles begins with a single step" and be patient with yourself if the changes you make seem small and the process slow.

"Putting our cards on the table" -- describing feelings, behaviors and thoughts openly -- can help us make the small decisions that lead to long-term positive change. One person might recognize that working long hours is putting his health in jeopardy. Another might see that not working long enough hours is putting his or her family's financial well-being at risk. Someone else might, of necessity, work long hours, neglecting to take some special time with her child. Competing demands of work and family often obscure our valid needs for personal time, leisure pursuits and community activities. We all have the same 24 hours each day and need regular check-ups, both on our emotional state in the moment and on the overall balance in our lives.

Family life is under tremendous stress in contemporary society and it is a serious challenge to find -- or make -- time for it. What can we do less of in order to spend more time with each other? One suggestion is to turn the TV off at least one evening or one full day a week. That is one thing anyone can do to reclaim family time. But there are many things in our lives over which we have no control: You or a family member may become ill or recover from an illness, lose a job or get a new one. Negative and positive changes -- gains and losses -- can be almost equally disruptive. External changes in our family situation require us to change. Recalling the handy guide, our first tool, you can see that as your family situation changes, you will need to reassess your time budget:

- When your children are very young, your time for community service is limited. As they get older, their activities can give you opportunities for service, like coaching a sport or leading a scout troop. Perhaps, however, something that also gives you time away from family members would refresh your spirit more.

- If you haven't contacted a dear uncle or sister in a while, maybe you need to take time to call or write him or her. Perhaps arranging for your children to visit grandparents would give everyone a much-needed change.

- It may have been too long since you took time to play, thinking mistakenly that it is less important than work. How about ten minutes for a quick catch or round of "hangman" (a spelling game) between dinner and homework time?

- Has your work become a bore or an overwhelming challenge? Is there a positive change you could consider in this area? What about regularly swapping some duties with a coworker? Many companies now organize their workforce into teams to do just this.

- This shouldn't be last, but have you been taking good care of yourself? You get to decide what it means to do this! A break could be 15 minutes for a crossword puzzle (my personal favorite). Small changes mean a great deal.

Whether you are under stress or not -- and most parents are, some of the time -- it is helpful to spend a few minutes at least once or twice a week using these three tools to evaluate your feelings about what's going on in your life. In doing so you will see more clearly the problems you face and, with any luck, discover choices you didn't realize you had. Perhaps you need a walk, either alone or with the kids just for fun. Ask them to take you to the park! Turning the tables this way can offer a welcome, humorous break from the stress that comes with being the grownup. Of course, as a parent you will have to set guidelines for the role reversal. If your four-year-old is going to take a turn making dinner, the meal might be carrot sticks and peanut butter crackers, but nobody needs to go to bed hungry. And you don't have to cook.

Perhaps it's service that's lacking in your life. Doing a kindness for an elderly neighbor or for a younger parent would refresh your spirit. Only you can tell what you need and want in your life. And you can tell what you need and want only if you know how you feel. Keep the conversational formula in your mind, just the way you keep the thermometer on hand to take your child's temperature.

Unfortunately, the conversational formula does not guarantee results, either at home or in a public situation. If you tell someone who cuts ahead of you at the grocery checkout, "I feel disrespected by your cutting in line because I have been waiting my turn," they may say, "Well, too bad, I was here first!" or they may respond, "Oh, sorry, go ahead." You may -- or may not -- get the response you want. Whether you speak up or not, and whether the response is what you desire or not, the discipline of clarifying one's feelings is nevertheless useful. Recognizing how you feel can relieve your stress at the time, even if all you do is make a mental note to talk over an annoyance or anxiety later with a friend. In becoming familiar with the three tools described above, you are getting ready to use the eight questions that constitute our agenda. The power of the tools and these eight questions lies in the self-

Once it took me three days to muster the courage to do so, but I made an appointment with a supervisor and told her I was uncomfortable with the way she had spoken to me in a meeting. I didn't "tell her off." I didn't expect an apology and I didn't get one. I simply used the conversational formula, saying that I felt insulted, that I enjoyed the job and valued our working relationship. I can't say that it became perfect overnight, but it improved. There certainly were no more insults in meetings.

knowledge you acquire through using them, not in achieving control over your children. The example we set through our own behavior is a crucial component of our parenting. We must take time to carefully examine our expectations, motivations, and actions. The questions help us do this.

Questions, Not Answers

Chapter Five

Because people have been raising children forever, you might think the process should come naturally. But our instincts take us only so far. Parenting today involves everything from feeding and changing our new-born infant to helping our teenager with homework for a biology course only distantly related to the one we may have taken twenty, thirty or forty years ago. Our children, as young adults, may need more guidance -- on personal, educational, career or financial decisions — than we can possibly provide. We need a range of skills that at times can be staggering, but we can feel less overwhelmed and can gain both inspiration and instruction if we share experiences with other parents.

Some child-rearing practices date from an era when children were considered property, and behaviors fostered by this power structure persist in families today, sometimes openly, sometimes subtly. While we no longer "own" our children, we are still the heads of our families. As such, we are rightly powerful. But with the immense power we have in our children's lives comes the obligation to consider how we use it. While we respect the many differences in parenting styles and practices, the PARENTS FORUM approach is based on a fundamental concern that parenting serve children's best interests.

The eight questions of our agenda serve as starting points for individual reflection and for mutually supportive discussion among parents. Many of us find too few chances to talk with other parents, and the rare opportunities we have are often rushed. There is simply no substitute for face-to-face conversation, as the spirited discussions that take place at school bus stops and among parents attending children's performances and games demonstrate!

We consider each of these eight questions in turn in PARENTS FORUM workshops, but you can also tackle them outside the workshop format with a friend or family member. As we do this, it is helpful to remember that good parenting is a process, not a goal. We won't be able to give our kids every joy or help them avoid every anxiety that we've experienced — we wouldn't want to. Our kids need us to be there emotionally for them, applauding when they succeed and sympathizing when they fail at the large and small tasks of growing up. At the same time, gradually and more or less gracefully, we need to let them become independent, even as we hold fast to the love and duty that keep families together. What to do? And when?

Experts offer conflicting advice. As a result, we may feel we are on a pendulum swinging between too permissive and too harsh, asking one day "Was I strict enough?" and the next day "Was I too strict?" Our goal in PARENTS FORUM is to help each other strike a good balance between the two extremes, creating consistency while allowing flexibility in response to our children's changing needs. We approach that elusive happy medium in discipline in part by changing the way we communicate with our children.

At its core, this change involves replacing general questions like 'How are you doing?" with more specific ones like "What was the best thing that happened today? "What was the worst?" "Did you have fun in art class?" "How did that spelling test, soccer game or swim meet go?" When we ask about people and events our kids have already mentioned, they know that we have been listening and they realize that we are interested in them and in what's going on in their lives. By our example, we can help them become interested in other people and show them how to express that interest.

This chapter will guide you through the eight questions as they are presented in a PARENTS FORUM workshop and will illustrate ways that other parents have found them helpful. It is a good idea to consider all the questions on the easy days, when you are not under stress, so that you will be able to call up the relevant question on the inevitable rough days. Everyone has at least a few rough days! In the midst of a conflict with my children (and yes, I still have "push-pulls" with them even though they are living on their own), often ask myself what question might help resolve the conflict, or at least point toward a resolution. For example, is the problem about a concern (question two), or values (question four) or rules (question five)? Does the situation involve leaving or letting go (question seven) or change (question eight)? Specifically, does the situation call for a change on my part? Once

Upon returning to the paid workforce when my two older boys were in primary school, I sometimes arrived home after they did. The first words out of their mouths, as I drove up in the car or walked through the door, were usually, "Hi, Mom, what's for dinner?" It was an important milestone when one of the boys -- about ten years old at the time -- asked instead, "Hi, Mom, how was your day?" He hesitated only a second or two before continuing... "What's for dinner?" but still, it was a start! He asked about my day -- even if he didn't wait for the answer that first time -- and showed a new awareness: Mom is a person with friends, work, a life, outside the home. Now they ask informed questions, "How's your boss doing?" or "What's going on with your friend Bonny?" We should recognize our children as individuals and they can learn to return the favor. It's wonderful when they do.

you have worked through all eight questions, you can select the one most useful in a specific instance.

Workshops consider the questions in a number of meetings from eight separate sessions to a single session. There are two specific benefits to participating in a workshop. First, you take time away from your family and gain perspective simply from being away. A workshop serves as a mini-retreat. Second, you get the benefit of other people's perspectives on similar situations in their own lives and, if you ask for it, the benefit of their advice.

However, you can also consider the questions on your own or informally with your spouse or a small group of friends. Try to set aside some time, perhaps when your children have gone to bed or early in the morning before they wake up, to answer the questions, writing your answers down if you like. If possible, set aside some time with your spouse or a trusted friend to share your answers. You can also raise them in conversation with your children, other adults in your family or friends.

Your answers may be different from one day to another and your understanding will probably deepen as you spend more time on each question. You may find new insights each time you go through the series, so it can be useful to work through them more than once and save your responses to compare, over time.

An important element in the success of your conversations with others -- and a key to a successful workshop -- is a firm commitment to confidentiality. I will more easily share concerns with you if you assure me that you will not talk about them to

other people. A second concern regarding confidentiality is whether issues raised by one person in a discussion should, or should not, be raised by the other person at another time. Agreements about confidentiality should be clear. It is a good idea to mention one's concern for confidentiality at the start of a conversation and it doesn't hurt for people to remind each other at the end of the conversation as well. I might say, after telling a friend something that's troubling me, "Please don't mention this to anyone else and please wait for me to bring it up again." Or "Please don't mention this to anyone else, but it's okay to ask me about it -- I need the support."

There are situations, though, where safety is concerned and the listener should seriously consider breaking confidentiality. If a friend is talking about suicide or behaving in ways that threaten their own or another's safety, it is essential to seek help. There are 24-hour "hotlines" with staff and volunteers who welcome calls from friends and family members concerned about someone close to them. Also, there are public and private agencies that offer mental health

Some years back one of my sons (a teenager at the time) confided to me that he felt as if life were no longer worth living. My first response was to discount his concern, but, feeling desperate and helpless, I forced myself just to sit with him. I asked him to tell me if he really meant what he said, what other thoughts he had, what plans he had considered or possibly made. Finally recognizing that he was serious, I knew I had to call for help. I called The Samaritans, a suicide prevention hotline, and spoke with the volunteer on the line. Then I handed the telephone to my son. He spoke with the volunteer for a few minutes and handed the phone back to me. The person on the other end of the line-- a lifeline, for sure -- urged me to take my son to the hospital and

services. You may need support or advice yourself in order to advise or support a person close to you who is suffering acutely or who is at risk of endangering themselves or someone else.

In Massachusetts, where I live, certain professionals, teachers and others in human services, have the status of "mandated reporter." As such, they are obliged to report suspected incidents of abuse or neglect of children. As volunteers, PARENTS FORUM participants and coordinators are not mandated reporters. The benefit of this non-professional status is that others may feel more open in speaking with us. Our responsibility, as volunteers, is to honor the trust people place in us. When appropriate, we urge participants to seek professional help if we see that their concerns are outside the normal range or that the reassurance we offer appears inadequate to their level of distress.

If we were in a workshop now, the facilitator would say, "Let's get started," and would ask you to turn to the PARENTS FORUM agenda. Here it is:

did. That hospitalization was the first of several and he whole story is long and complicated. His depression had a slow onset and probably a number of causes. Several months before he had suffered the loss, to suicide, of a beloved teacher. Her death cannot be called the cause of his thoughts of suicide, but it certainly affected both of us deeply. The point of sharing this painful incident with you is to show how, in a moment when all I wanted was to turn away from distress, mine and his, I chose to face it and ask for help. I got help for myself so that I could get my son the help he so desperately needed. He's okay today, thanks to the volunteers and the professionals who helped him and helped me.

Getting Acquainted
1. What do you like about your family?
2. What concerns or troubles you about your family?
3. How do you express concern to a family member? How do you ask for and give advice and/or help in your family and community?

Getting Organized
4. What are your household values?
5. What are your household rules?

Getting Serious
6. What happens when someone joins your family?
7. What happens when someone leaves your family?

Stating Changes
8. What changes have you experienced recently? What changes do you expect in the future?

The following paragraphs describe how we present these questions in our workshops and share some of the responses participants have given. You may find some of the examples of family discord trivial, or even silly. This is precisely the point. If we consider minor concerns and our feelings about them, we develop skills for dealing with the major concerns and have a better chance of avoiding emotional blowups.

1. What do you like about your family?

In answering the first question under the topic Getting Acquainted, "What do you like about your family?" stay specific. Picture a happy time in the recent or distant past. Describe your feelings about the family gathering or event and about the people involved. Practice using the conversational formula, "I feel... (or I felt...) about...

because...." It may be more difficult than you realize to do this, as we may take happiness for granted. We do this exercise for its own sake and because recognition and affirmation of the positive elements in our relationships give us courage to face conflicts when they arise.

Time spent answering this question can help remedy that unfortunate family condition "Appreciation Deficit Disorder." If we remind ourselves to appreciate each other more -- more often and more openly -- we may find our family life improving and our satisfaction with our family life increasing. Saying specifically what we enjoy may be as challenging as "getting down and dirty" with what we dislike. When we give our kids and our spouses or partners informative praise, they know what to do more of. "Thanks for setting the table." "That sweater -- or shirt -- or haircut -- looks great!" "I noticed you made the bed and opened the shades -- the bedroom looks great." My two favorites in this category are, "Gee, Mom, you look great!" and "Lunch was delicious. May I help with the dishes?" although I confess that the second is not original to me.

Describing happy family moments and taking the time to express love and appreciation to family members provides a welcome antidote to the negativity we and our children sometimes too easily fall into. Children are more likely to express positive feelings if they hear their fathers and mothers and other important people in their lives doing so. Think back to a family picnic, or a day at the beach, when your kids had a great time and fell asleep in the car on the way home, giving you a full 45 minutes of adult conversation. Remember how peaceful and appreciative you felt. Reminisce about these pleasant moments, even when, or especially when, they are followed by less than happy landings as these same children, still sandy, but now awake and cranky, have to be given baths and put unwillingly to bed. Oh, those transitions. Remember to breathe.

> *A couple involved in our program, asked how they were different from their own parents, responded that they frequently tell their kids they love them. The husband remarked that he often says, "I love you" to his son and, ruefully, described his own father's discomfort at hearing him say, "I love you, Dad." This couple said that while they happily do many of the same things their parents did, they realize that the parenting they got is not all the parenting they want to give, particularly when it comes to communication.*

The shift from happy recollections to troublesome ones is natural enough, though. Most people benefit from a chance to complain. It feels like letting off steam, a relief. In a PARENTS FORUM workshop, we move to our second question, which gives us just that opportunity.

2. What concerns or troubles you about your family?

The second Getting Acquainted question, "What concerns or troubles you about your family?" faces the negativity head-on. Use the same formula, "I feel... about... because...." to describe a family issue that concerns you now. You can define family as the people you are presently living with, spouse, children or housemates, or you may define your family more broadly to include siblings, parents, children who may live elsewhere. You can pick a small annoyance (your ten-year-old or your spouse not hanging the bathmat on the edge of the tub after taking a shower) or a major worry (your mother's illness and diminishing capacity to care for herself).

For as long as you can, or as long as is useful to clarify your feelings, stay with the annoyance or worry without rushing to what might happen next or what you might do to remedy the situation. Our society is fast-paced and we tend to hurry. Emotions do not fare well under pressure. Just as we slow down for the good stuff in answering the first question, we slow down for the not-so-good stuff as well as for the down-right difficult.

In a group discussion we move directly from this question to the next, but if you are working through these questions on your own, you might want to take the time to write down your concerns and your feelings about them. You may find it helpful to keep the list handy as you read the next section and consider what, if anything, to do about one or another of your concerns.

3. How do you express concern to a family member? How do you ask for and give advice and/or help in your family and community?

This last Getting Acquainted question is really three in one: "How do you express concern? How do you ask for and receive advice? How do you ask for and give help?" This set of questions offers a bridge between feeling concern (which comes up with question two) and expressing it. Notice the different elements within these questions: Under "expressing concern" the concern could be about oneself or about another family member, and could be expressed directly to the person or to someone else close to that person. Under "asking for advice and help" we look at our own willingness to receive, and under "giving advice and help" we look at our willingness to speak up to others and our ability to seek out needed services and advocate for them.

In answering this three-in-one question, we consider the range of choices we have once we know what our concerns are. We may choose to do nothing. The concern may be none of our business and we may need only to talk with a friend who can be trusted to honor our confidence. We may wish to talk the concern over, in confidence, and then speak with the family member we are concerned about. We might offer some advice or help, or suggest seeking help from outside the family. It is important to recognize the continuum from concern to advice to help and -- just as important -- to pause before going from one to the next.

When I have a concern about one of my children or another family member, it can help to take some time before rushing to talk or advise or help. A situation may resolve itself. Or a night's rest and a new day may

give me a better idea of how to approach the situation. One friend has a 24-hour rule: if a conflict arises with someone outside the immediate family, she waits one day before acting -- or reacting!

In our workshops, we do a brief role-play -- and you can do this in your head or with another adult -- a "before and after" exchange of this nature. For the "before PARENTS FORUM" version, you can exaggerate a worst case, an attack of the screaming meemies.

In my family, the Bathmat Issue is a classic, trivial yet persistent source of conflict. I found it annoying to have to straighten the bathroom up, and put the bathmat back on the edge of the tub, after my teenage son had showered. He was quite capable of the task but I could not force him to do it. I'd start by telling him, honestly, that I felt annoyed. I might mention that I appreciated his helpfulness in setting the dinner table -- he's basically responsible -- and I'd ask him how he could remember to do that little chore. If I were feeling patient,

Your kids didn't clean up their playroom and, yelling, you punish them with "No TV for a week!" The "after PARENTS FORUM" version might be, "Susie, I feel disappointed about your not putting your blocks away because I reminded you about cleaning up before dinner."

Instead of an unrelated punishment, no television, you could impose a natural consequence, "We'll give these blocks a week's 'vacation' and get them out again when you can follow through on putting things away after you play." This inspired solution to the messy play-room problem came out of a workshop discussion. The report from the parents who tried it is that it worked!

In the before-and-after role-play, one participant volunteers to describe a difficult situation involving concern, advice, or help that he or she faces. The participant may take an active role or may ask others to do so. With the volunteer facilitator as director, the participants act out the situation. Applause is allowed! The facilitator then asks for comments, first from the players involved, "How did that feel to you? Did you accomplish what you wanted?" then from the observers, "Did that look successful? Would you have said or done something else in that situation?" The role-play may be repeated, if time allows, with a different situation or a new cast.

might ask if he needed my help, that is, a reminder, next time. If I were feeling frustrated, I might tell him that if he forgot again, I'd impose some consequence, like an extra chore, perhaps cleaning the bathroom. When my son moved back to live with his father, the problem was solved, at least in my house. In any case, he had learned that small household issues can mean a lot and that it's important to have clear rules and good communication about them, so they stay small.

Still on the continuum of question three -- concern, advice and help -- we present a technique called bookending: When a workshop participant needs to have a difficult conversation with someone, we suggest that they first talk with a sympathetic friend or another parent. They then go ahead and have the conversation or confrontation. Finally they review it, afterwards, with the sympathetic friend. Some examples of situations that might be made easier by such 'bookending' are given below. Note the progression from less serious to more serious intervention.

- talking with your child or the mother of your child's classmate about a missing (possibly stolen?) plaything

- asking a teacher for advice in helping your son discourage or counter his classmate's bullying, or asking her to change your child's seating because of the bullying

- asking a school administrator to change your child's class if the teacher was not successful in handling the situation involving bullying

Any of these conversations can be difficult and the outcomes uncertain. I find such conversations less stressful if I prepare for them with a friend and can anticipate reviewing them with the same friend afterwards, in effect putting support "bookends" around them. In asking a friend, neighbor or coworker for support of this kind, it's important to be respectful. It's good to give the person the option of declining. They might not have time or might simply not want to be involved. You can say, "I'm having a problem with my child -- or sibling -- or spouse -- or boss. Could you give me your perspective on the situation?" Be sure to ask, "Is this a good time?" If the time isn't right, but they want to listen, you can set another time, and a limited time, to talk.

Afterwards, of course, say thank you. If you are the person who listened, you can say thanks, as well, for the trust your friend has placed in you. If you ask a friend to help you rehearse a difficult conversation -- perhaps the example above, calling your child's class- mate's mother about something the classmate might have taken -- report back to that friend afterwards. This second "bookend" gives you a chance to consider how the conversation went and shows your friend courtesy too -- he or she is probably curious about the end of the story!

The ordinary complications of our lives, losing or changing a job, moving to a new house and changing schools, not to mention the extraordinary but too-fre- quent complications of divorce, serious illness, or death, bring up intense feelings. Such events give us opportunities, either welcome or unwelcome, to share concern and ask for advice or help. If we begin learn- ing to ask for and accept help early on, when our kids are little, the process will get easier and over time we

A friend, the mother of young children, told me how she talked to a neighbor about a problem she was having with her husband. It was a personal prob- lem, something she wouldn't share with just any- one. She termed it "serious, but not divorce-type stuff" that had, nonetheless, left her exhausted and desperate. The neighbor listened and then revealed she had experienced the same thing. Surprised and relieved at the outset, my friend went on to have a very productive and profound discussion with her neighbor, one that was very helpful to both of them.

will build a network of friends with whom we exchange help. The primary benefit of this process is to us, as parents. Other people's ideas, time and energy can be of immense help. A secondary benefit is to our children. We are setting good examples for them.

We now move on to the next section of the agenda, two more questions on the nitty-gritty of household management.

Getting Organized
4. What are your household values?
5. What are your household rules?

As the workshop moves from Getting Acquainted to the next topic, Getting Organized, we present a diagram that shows four parenting styles. The volunteer facilitator presents this so-called "algebra lesson" before moving on to the questions in this section.

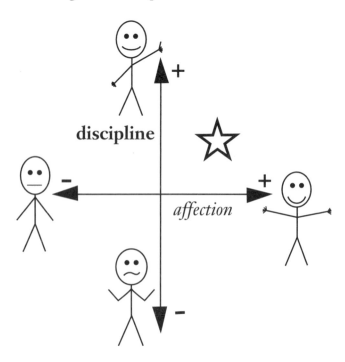

The diagram helps us clarify the parenting style we use in communicating our values and rules to our children and helps us identify the effectiveness of different styles in different situations.

Different proportions of affection and discipline characterize these four parenting styles. Using the diagram as a reference, workshop participants are asked to share stories about people in their lives, during either childhood or adulthood, who characterize different aspects of these four styles. For example:

- your dad, who taught you subtraction when the nuns at school said you'd never learn

- your grandfather whose unconditional love helped you through the loss of a parent

- a demanding coach who went too far, insisting that you finish practice even though you were injured

- an inattentive teacher who let you slide by with less than your best effort.

Doing this exercise on your own is fine, but doing it with someone else can be especially beneficial, as each person's reminiscences encourage the other's. Think about adults whose affection and discipline made a difference in your early life and describe how they showed their care. Did adults in your family have defined roles, with one usually a "toughie" and the other a "softy"? Then think of times when you, as a parent, have been affectionate or demanding with your children. Ask yourself, or ask each other, what made you choose the "softer" or "tougher" approach.

Can you imagine having more flexibility in your parenting, being -- from time to time -- more or less affectionate and/or more or less demanding? Your children need both affection and discipline, of course. The challenge is to discern how much of each they need and when! We get better understanding of our choices if we look again at the "algebra lesson" and consider an important element in affection -- inquiry -- along with an important element in discipline -- advocacy.

Affection does not exist in a vacuum. People cannot have deep feelings for each other without knowing each other and the process of getting acquainted involves a lot of asking and telling: one person expressing interest and listening to the other person's answers. If we want to get and stay acquainted with our children over time, or with any family member or friend for that matter, we have to ask them questions. That's how inquiry supports and enhances affection.

Discipline does not exist in a vacuum either. Parents can get only so far with "Because I said so." We can be

> A defiant four-year-old challenged her mother, "I am so mad I could pour this milk over your head!" Her mother, completely out of patience, said, "That gives me an idea," and proceeded to pour milk over the girl's head. This memorably disrespectful moment from my own childhood was retold many times for humorous effect, but I recall it with sadness and remember the retelling more clearly than the actual confrontation. What was she thinking? Evidently she wasn't thinking clearly. If my mother's failure of self-control makes you wince, well, there are a few incidents from my own parenting that make me do the same, and perhaps one or two from yours as well. My mother could have taken a minute to ask me why I was angry and then responded. Her reaction to my challenge was remarkable for its absence of both inquiry and advocacy.

more effective in offering or limiting choices and in setting consequences if we have well thought-out reasons for our rules and if we explain both the reasons and the rules clearly. That's how advocacy -- effectively communicating the rationale behind our actions -- supports and enhances discipline. Like affection and discipline, inquiry and advocacy complement each other and are most effectively used in partnership with each other.

The importance of affection and the necessity of discipline are both obvious: our children need us to love them and need us to guide them. The notions of inquiry and advocacy may be a little more difficult to grasp.

The terms come from a workshop I took at MIT on group process where they were used to describe the two types of behavior a participant may show in a discussion. The advocacy stance, like the disciplinarian's, comes with a raised voice, perhaps a raised or pointed finger, explaining, showing the right way. In a parent's voice, advocacy can be, "You should do this! You shouldn't do that!" "This is right! That's wrong!" and most important, "This is why." Discipline, in adequate doses -- teaching and modeling appropriate behavior -- is essential to good parenting, of course. Effective parents stand for something, but we need to temper our advocacy with inquiry. "What is going on?" "Do you think that is a good idea?" "How can you settle that disagreement?" "Do you need my help right now?" A parent using advocacy in the extreme becomes dictatorial and a parent using inquiry in the extreme turns into a doormat. We've all seen parents who give a young child too many choices! Figuring out how much to ask and how much to tell is not easy, even if one has settled the twin issues of what to ask and what to tell.

Further complicating a parent's job is the fact that the balance between advocacy and inquiry is bound to change as a young person moves through childhood into adolescence, shifting more toward inquiry. "What happened? How did you feel? When did you decide to do that (for example, to misbehave)? Who was with you? Would you do the same thing again?" Advocacy has a kind of built-in, reinforcement for a parent --

I recently came across notes I had written on a New Year's Eve several years ago about a distressing incident involving one of my sons. He was living at his dad's house and was supposed to be out with friends. He certainly did not have permission to have company at my house. When I arrived home at 10:30, after ushering at a concert, I found him there with two girls, both his classmates, and one guy who was the older brother of one of the girls.

The stage was set for either a big lecture on choices and consequences regarding alcohol and other drugs, or screaming and yelling about rules and punishments: "This is a sober home. Drinking at your age is both dangerous and illegal." But, surprising myself, I chose a response with some advocacy, certainly, but more weighted toward inquiry, either out of shock or sadness. I managed to keep a low tone of voice and I hope I may even have sounded gracious to my son's friends, one of whom I had never met. "This is not acceptable. You need to leave now. I am very disappointed. It's cold. I'll drive you home. Please clean the counter now. Tomorrow you will come back and clean the floor."

I was furious, but I didn't yell. I clearly expressed my disapproval, disappointment and concern. According to my notes -- and the fact that I wrote notes at all reveals the progress I'd made in becoming more thoughtful and deliberate as a parent-- I called my ex-husband and the mother of one of the girls.

"I'm doing my job; I am the adult here!" -- so it can be tempting to over-use it, despite the fact that, ultimately, inquiry may be more effective. If I say something in a convincing and assertive tone, the sound of my words tells me I'm right, even if what I say doesn't convince my child. Inquiry, on the other hand, can be

---

My son and one of the girls were quite clearly intoxicated or high and I repeatedly urged them to let me drive them home. They refused but assured me that they would go directly home, a walk of only a few blocks. I let them go. Was that the right thing to do? I'm not sure. I remember feeling angry and helpless at the same time but relieved to be able to contact the other parents concerned. Looking back I'm not sure if this episode should go in the 'loss' or the 'win' column. Maybe it was a tie: a loss in that it happened at all and a win in that I handled it calmly.

I guess the reason I wrote things down was to be able to be clear about what happened when I talked to my son the next day about his blatant disrespect for my house rules and about his lack of concern for his and his friends' health and safety.

Probably I could have done more inquiry at the time. I certainly did the next day, when I again called my ex-husband and the parents of the other young people. That night it seemed as if I wouldn't get sensible answers to the questions I wanted to ask, "Who got the alcohol? Where did the marijuana come from?" so I let them go, both the questions and the young people. How different that exchange was from earlier years when another son acted out in similar ways, and we lashed out at each other verbally. I still regret those "first drafts" at parenting.

frustrating for a parent, as it opens the door to challenge or at least a different view. Asking my son a question about his behavior (or misbehavior!) may be more difficult than telling him right off the bat what I think and what I think he should do, but doing so may lead him to share information or feelings that could help me respond more effectively to the situation.

The choice between advocacy and inquiry can be a tough call. As the chapter title promised, PARENTS FORUM gives you questions, not answers, and suggests ways you can evaluate your parenting on an ongoing basis. If you catch yourself "advocating up a storm," yelling or arguing forcefully to shut off challenge from your child, it's good to notice what you are doing and consider whether it is working. If you take the other tack and try a strong dose of inquiry, the same holds true. Ask yourself if what you did worked for you and for your kid, in that situation. Ask your young person the same thing, not giving them the authority to decide how you should behave as a parent, but asking them, perhaps, "Was what I did or what I said helpful to you?

A key to determining whether a child needs more discipline or affection, more advocacy or inquiry, is his or her developmental stage. People who study on-the-job training for adults have identified four stages involved in learning any new task. Margaret Ann Gray, a staff development specialist at MIT where I work, characterized these stages by giving them animal names: puppy, snail, donkey and eagle. In a workshop on how to effectively manage volunteers, she describes a new volunteer as a puppy, a somewhat experienced volunteer as a snail, a more experienced but not yet fully competent volunteer as a donkey, and the 'ace' volunteer as an eagle.

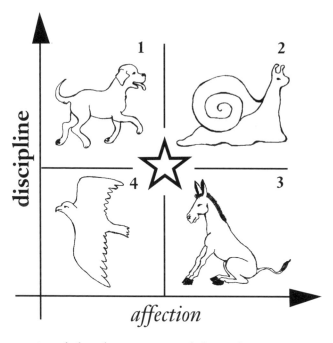

I was struck by the aptness of these images to young people's development. A little kid has many of the attitudes and behaviors -- as well as the appeal -- of a puppy. A school-age child, like a snail, seems to take forever doing the simplest things. I recall a dad at my sons' school once saying his fourth-grade daughter took so long to complete a task that waiting for her to finish was like "watching paint dry." Then there is the teenager, stubborn as a donkey, who really needs more carrot and less stick, more encouragement and less direction. Why didn't anyone tell me this before?! It would have spared my teenagers and me considerable grief. The eagle image is clear, too, of course. We want our young adult children to take wing and fly on their own.

Yet even our grown children sometimes need our direction and encouragement and we want to give both when we can. I certainly look forward to having my sons visit their childhood 'nest' from time to time, even after they've built, or rented, their own. Parents in many cultures expect young adults to live in the family home for extended periods. One of my sons recently moved back home for a few weeks and we had to talk through our understanding so that the arrangement felt like moving forward, not back, to both of us.

In PARENTS FORUM workshops, participants are asked how they have balanced discipline with affection at their children's different stages of development by sharing anecdotes that illustrate their own parenting strategies, both successful and unsuccessful. Discussions can get quite animated, as parents describe progress through their own developmental stages. A current adage says that good judgment comes from experience and experience comes from bad judgment. We can learn from each other and perhaps avoid some of the more serious misjudgments and mistakes.

It's all well and good to understand that a toddler learning to use the toilet or to put on his jacket will go through these four stages. It is helpful to know that the six-or seven-year old learning to set the table, ride a bike, or do addition, will also go through these stages. We can even see the adolescent venturing into the world of dating and the world of work behaving, in turn, like a puppy, snail, donkey and eagle. What may be less apparent -- yet equally important -- is the fact that we, as parents, go through similar stages. To many of us, parenting seemed relatively easy and fun at the beginning, even if the hours were long. As the kids got a little older, the job got harder and seemed endless. Finally, when I had worked through my insecurities and resentments, the donkey stage, and was beginning to feel confident and ready to soar, OH NO, my child had progressed to a new stage and needed me to start all over -- it seemed -- to develop a different parenting style.

It may be helpful to set aside some time to reflect on your own experiences with discipline and affection in your childhood, as well as in your adult work life and your parenting. Think, for example, of a time when someone was especially clear and encouraging in explaining something to you. Think of a time when the encouragement you wanted was not forthcoming from a parent, teacher, or boss. Think of a time when you "hit the right note" with a child in your life. You knew you gave him or her exactly the right "dose" of whatever he or she needed. It is just as important to remember the positive experiences as it is to be honest about the negative ones. In workshops, participants share both successes and struggles.

Workshop facilitators are asked to thank each person for whatever they say, without repeating, rephrasing or commenting on what the person said. If someone asks for feedback, of course, it can be given, but it is not imposed. Quiet participants are thanked also. Listening is as essential to our workshops as talking.

At this point, in a workshop, we acknowledge the work participants have done so far in going through these questions. Why not take a break before going on to the next section of our agenda? We do break here in our workshops.

4. What are your household values?

In Getting Organized, we consider two questions separately. You might find it difficult to answer question four, on values, without linking these to rules, but we make a distinction, as values presumably stay constant while rules need to change as your children grow. If we were talking together, doubtless we would come up with some basic, universal values: cleanliness, honesty, and good citizenship.

In workshops, a volunteer facilitator asks participants to write several values they consider important on a small card and collects the cards. The facilitator reads several or all of the cards (without indicating who wrote what) and asks people to comment, if they wish, describing how the value is demonstrated in their family. For example, "good nutrition" might elicit the comment, "I usually serve water, milk or juice to my kids instead of soda." "Honesty" ... "My kid returned a wallet to its owner." "Kindness" ... "My neighbor puts my trash bins in for me on trash day." "Responsibility" ... "I encourage my children to take good care of their pet."

The exercise of writing down values is a good one for a couple or a family to do together. The exercise may reveal conflicting values that underlie conflicts we experience when we interact with other people. It may also help clarify conflicts that arise between important values.

A classic conflict is between kindness and honesty. Do you tell a family member or friend that he's gained or lost a lot of weight? It may be true that he has, but you may feel uncomfortable, thinking it unkind, to tell him so. Yet your friendship may be one that can accommodate or that even demands such honesty. These issues are ones that you may not have thought about or discussed. You may find that there isn't necessarily agreement among family members, but the discussion can give you insight into the conflicts you experience.

What about conflicts between play and work, both important? What if I want to watch television (the value of enjoyment) and you think I should be folding laundry (the values of keeping the house in good order and being nicely dressed for school or work)? Maybe that's too easy! Of course you can fold laundry while watching television. But can your child do homework and watch television at the same time? Conflicts can arise over countless issues, large and small. So we clarify the values, as well as the feelings, behind our behaviors in order to more carefully and effectively "pick our battles."

Two more values that may conflict are neatness and creativity. If both are important to you, you might consider when and how these clash and then re-write your household rules accordingly. A sewing, painting, cooking or carpentry project might completely take over one room in the house or apartment. Who did the project? Who gets annoyed? Who cleans up? If you like to do creative projects yourself and want to promote creativity in your children, you might decide to "surrender and not scream at the messes," as one mother said. You could set boundaries on the creativity, that is, the messiness, in space and/or time, confining projects to a playroom table to be straightened up at least once a week. If we take some time to get clear in our own minds about what's important and what's realistic, we are much more likely to establish effective rules and to get our kids to follow them.

5. What are your household rules?

After values, we consider rules. This can be difficult. Two parents may agree on values but disagree on rules, as can parents and grandparents. But even if you disagree on values, you may find you can agree on some basic rules, if for different reasons. Often, we realize that we have never really examined or clarified the issues of values or rules, for ourselves individually, as a couple, or as a family.

If your family or household members are willing, after writing a list of the values you share, you can start trying to figure out what the actual rules are. Does mom or dad do all the cooking (yard work, animal care, driving or car repair) or are jobs shared? Who does the food shopping? Is it dad or mom who reads bedtime stories or do they take turns? Who washes the bathtub and who balances the checkbook? Who buys and wraps birthday and holiday presents? Who decides how much money to spend on necessities, entertainment, gifts, vacation trips and holiday celebrations? Who shops for what? Who cleans what? What responsibilities do children have at what ages?

Probably more important than any individual rule are these considerations: Who decides who does what? How are rules made in your household? How are they changed? How do people know if the rules have changed? While these questions are fundamental, they are seldom discussed. We tend to deal with issues as they come up, day to day.

If punctuality is important to me, what time should my teenager be home on weeknights? Parents need to be clear on their absolute values and at the same time be ready, from time to time, to negotiate changes in the rules. As just mentioned, we need to give some thought to when and how the rules get suspended or permanently changed. For example, a 13-year-old wants to sleep over at a friend's house on a weeknight and the rule is that sleepovers are allowed only on weekends. The parent might allow a suspension of the rule if the child asks in advance and there is a special reason, like a school outing the next day.

Of course, mom or dad may have different answers, so parents have to coordinate with each other, as much as they can, whether they are living together or not. Children often develop a keen sense of who decides what in a family, even when parents don't explicitly defer to one another. And when parents do this, responding "Ask your mother" or "Ask your

father" to a child's request, it can be helpful for the
parents to have a follow-up discussion. Even if your
spouse or partner is unwilling to devote time to talking
over these questions on values and rules, the process
is valuable for the parent who does it. He or she can
be clearer in his or her own mind about such issues
as these:

- Am I being consistent for the sake of consistency or my own convenience or am I perhaps
  abusing my authority -- "on a power trip"?

- Should I involve or not involve my child in
  negotiating an exception to a rule?

- If I make an exception will my child take it as
  a change in the rule?

- If I do change a rule, should the change be
  made on a trial basis for a specified period
  of time?

- If I uphold a rule and my child breaks it, do I
  impose reasonable consequences?

The conversational formula can be used anywhere in
the discussion to help family members understand
each other's points of view. The 13-year-old might say,
"I feel frustrated about your not letting me sleep over
at Janie's house because Rebecca's mother is letting
her sleep over" (a refined version of "All the kids are
doing it"). Mom might respond, "I feel anxious about
your wanting to sleep over because you won't get
enough rest to do well in school the next day or to
enjoy the outing" and might hold the line with a brief,
"No, you can't go." There might be a more serious reason to say no. Perhaps the mother is not confident
that parental supervision at the other home will be

adequate. A call to the other home, in that case, might reassure her or might confirm her decision to say no. On the other hand, the mother might express the same feeling but follow up with, "If you come home and take a nap the afternoon before, I will make an exception to the rule." The pattern we set for our own decision-making is one that our children often imitate, when they are done rebelling against it!

It can be helpful to write a values and rules statement  for your family. If you like, go back to the handy guide and write down a few values for each element of your life: self, relationships, achievement, leisure and service. Start with a few words on each element and describe the values or principles you hold and the rules or practices that follow from them. Include some principles you follow in caring for your home and possessions. It won't be etched in stone, of course. One page on the refrigerator is good enough.

Even if your family "mission statement" is very simple, it can be a helpful guide. If someone starts yelling, the person being yelled at can point out that a household value is kindness and that he, the "yellee," feels hurt or scared by the "yeller's" tone of voice. Just a suggestion. Remember this book did not promise answers, only questions.

As you think of the rules you make for your children, it may be helpful to think about the responsibilities you face as a parent. Your basic responsibility is to support your family. First and foremost you need to make sure, to the best of your ability, to provide food, clothing, shelter, access to medical care and access to educational opportunity for your children. Raising a child takes about twenty years and over those years, your job is re-defined each time your child learns to do something for himself. A newborn requires total care. A ten-year-old has doubtless learned to take responsibility for most basic necessities. A twenty-year-old may be living at home as a young adult or may be independent. The progression involves continual self-examination and re-evaluation of household rules. Family members may never be in complete agreement, but for a household to hold together, they have to reach some consensus.

We move on now to the next section of the agenda. In workshops, this is the halfway point and you can take it as a good time for a break. Put the book down. Breathe. Take a nap or a walk, if you can. Have a snack. Perhaps do some simple physical chore -- mow the lawn, walk the dog, fold the wash -- and let your mind wander over or away from the last five questions. You'll need to be refreshed to tackle the next two.

Getting Serious
6. What happens when someone joins your family?
7. What happens when someone leaves your family?

These questions help you look at the small and large transitions that occur in your family life. At the deepest level these are questions about birth and death and at the most superficial level they are about saying hello and good-bye. In workshops, we begin by describing intermediate transitions we have experienced ourselves: the first day of kindergarten and the last day of a school year or a summer camp experience. We think back to these and other changes we went through as children and young adults. Participants are encouraged to take time to reminisce with their kids and share these memories, both the lighter and often humorous ones, as well as more serious ones. In the workshops, as we consider these passages, we recall how we felt when they occurred.

Think of some beginnings ...remember your first day of kindergarten ...your first day in a new job or new school. Describe that experience using the conversational formula, "I felt / about / because /." Now recall that experience again mentioning something you or someone else did that helped you feel secure. Again, try using the phrase, "I felt / about / because /"

Then think of some endings ...remember your last day in grade school ...your high school graduation ...the end of a summer camp. Consider the experience twice, first describing the so-called negative feelings (sadness, regret, fear, uncertainty) and then the more positive feelings (pleasure, pride, relief, sense of accomplishment). Often there's both an upside and downside to our more memorable experiences, and our attitudes strongly influence the effect of these experiences on us. If we look at the negative aspects of an experience and acknowledge the feelings these provoke, we will be better able to see the positive aspects of the experience and more fully acknowledge and celebrate the good feelings these inspire.

From the first day of kindergarten through high school and college, to a new job, most of us wonder, "Will they like me? Can I do it? Will it be fun?" Recalling and acknowledging your own worries may help you to be more understanding of your child's present-day anxieties.

Deep emotions do come up in our workshops, of course. A participant in one of our early sessions described her grandmother's funeral, how desperate and lonely she felt at losing someone very, very dear and close to her. A participant in another workshop, recalling leaving her young daughter at day care, began crying. A father of preschoolers recalled his mother's recent death and was overcome with grief. PARENTS FORUM facilitators acknowledge that participants may experience very strong feelings as they answer these questions and affirm that this is an important part of the process.

If a participant brings up a serious current issue, a facilitator may ask him or her if they want some feedback or advice. When we give each other advice -- sometimes solutions to other peoples' problems are often easier to see than solutions to our own -- we try to present it, without pressure, in the form a question, "Have you considered...?" or "You might...." or "What about...?" We don't tell people what to do unless they specifically ask for suggestions (for example, sharing information about community resources) and generally we try to offer sympathy and empathy and share stories about how we have dealt with similar challenges.

Discussing these two Getting Serious questions with family members or a trusted friend may help you anticipate your own needs when transitions loom. The stages of our children's lives can bring up feelings of sadness and happiness both, as we mourn in some way the loss of our little kid and delight in our child's passing a new milestone. More than one dad has held back or shed some tears as he sees his daughter in her first prom gown. More than a few mothers have found the first day of kindergarten to be the occasion of a 'crying club.'

Of course, there are beginnings and endings every day. You can think of these two questions as "How do you say hello?" and "How do you say good-bye?" In today's busy life we are constantly leaving one place and the people there and arriving at another place where we interact with other people. Even when we are in one place all day, we experience beginnings and endings to parts of the day. A workshop I attended on effective meetings stressed the importance of allowing time at the beginning and end of each meeting for social conversation. The "small talk" might be on weather, sports, movies or simply casual conversation, even the inconsequential "How have you been?" as a lead-in to the "big talk" of the meeting. The leader of that workshop gave several examples, describing all of our interactions -- telephone conversations, chance in-person encounters at the market, even e-mail message exchanges -- as meetings that can benefit from a courteous "lead-in" and "lead-out."

An uncommon courtesy, one I appreciate when others offer it to me, is asking, especially when calling on the telephone, "Is this a good time?" I try to remember to ask this of others. When people of any age, children or adults, are given this choice they can usually listen more attentively. If we pay attention to the small transitions in our lives and try to make them with some grace, we may find it easier to meet the greater transitions we inevitably face in a similar manner.

Now, we move on to the last question.

Stating Changes
8. What changes have you experienced recently? What changes do you expect in the future?

The workshops close with a discussion of change and this is a two-in-one question, looking back, then forward. It is inevitable, of course. Becoming a parent, becoming a successful parent, means learning to deal with change and teaching our children to do so as well. There are all kinds of changes in our lives:

changes in ourselves, those in others, changes we anticipate with delight, those we dread, changes we share and those we accomplish or suffer alone. People change at different rates and sometimes the changes we make take us in different directions. An awareness of values, a sense of those values most dearly held, can be a life preserver in a sea of change.

The importance of the changes we experience in our lives becomes clear only if we first recognize them, then talk about them, and celebrate or lament them. We do this in our workshops and one special thing we do is make the end of each PARENTS FORUM workshop a graduation. We give certificates to everyone who has participated and we ask each person to give their own mini-valedictory on the topic of change.

Each of us wants to do a good job as a parent. We want to be happy and want the same for our spouse or partner, our parents, siblings, children, and our bosses and coworkers too. If we fully experience the

A newspaper reporter attended a one-day workshop, intending to sit outside the circle, observe and write about the process. We invited him to sit in, instead. Although not a parent himself, he spent the next several hours enthusiastically sharing his own experiences, thoughts and feelings, listening to others, commenting on the role plays, and finally giving his own short graduation speech. His perspectives on parenting, as a recent 'consumer' of parent 'services' were helpful to the parents of young children. His participation enriched the discussion for all of us.

changes we have to make in the course of our lives, and if we accept and manage in positive ways the anger, fear and sadness that come up along the way, we can more fully enjoy the happiness that life brings. A friend told me once that "Sorrow carves out so that joy may fill up."

The practices described above: considering feelings and thoughts and discussing them with other parents, along with asking the right questions, are the foundations of PARENTS FORUM. They help us see the shifting, sometimes fuzzy line between cherishing our children (good for them and for us) and coddling them (often not so good either for them or for us). The practices are useful whether you have an infant, a teenager, or children grown and gone. They are useful to you whether you live in a big city, a town, or open country, no matter what world you live in, New or Old, North or South, no matter whether you live in a developed or a developing country. Thoughtful, caring, mutually supportive discussions with other parents will help us become better guides for our children as they grow, grow up, and perhaps go on to create their own families.

Watch Your Words and Your Silences

Chapter Six

As parents, we risk passing along to our children the tension that we experience and we can, all too easily, let our kids' moods affect us as well. Patience wearing thin, a mother swears at her kids to "clean up the (expletive) playroom." With five minutes to go before the school bus arrives, another mom berates her daughter for misplacing her backpack, "What's wrong with you? Are you a dummy?" This chapter focuses on how we behave towards our children when we are tired, anxious, angry -- or all three -- and how we behave toward them when they are tired, anxious or angry. It suggests conversational safety valves that kids and parents alike can use.

It should be noted that our silences, like our words, deserve our attention, too. How many of us can remember, as children, talking to one of our parents and having mom or dad say, "I'm listening, go ahead..." without looking up from a newspaper or a cookbook? Can you remember how you felt? Unheard? Unconsidered? Unimportant?

With the stresses most parents experience, most of us have done this, at one time or another, with our children, spouse or partner. "Sure, sweetheart, I hear you," we may say when we're only half listening. We have good intentions. We start to listen, or may look as if we're listening, but in reality we're just waiting for the other person to stop talking so we can go back to whatever we were doing. "Using our words" both honestly and lovingly is half the work in building and maintaining any relationship; listening attentively is the other half.

Mastery of these crucial skills requires empathy, a quality defined in the dictionary as an "understanding of the situation, feelings and motives of another person." Imagine that each of us is born with our own internal "empathy account," and to the extent that others and we ourselves "make deposits" to this account we are able to "draw" on our reserves and extend empathy to others. Parents especially, who are called on daily to give good attention and understanding to their children, need to receive the same in order to maintain their "accounts." If family members or friends, in PARENTS FORUM or another supportive setting, listen to me without judging me when I need to talk about my worries and challenges, I will probably be better able to listen to my children. This talking and listening helps raise our emotional awareness. Emotional awareness, in turn, helps us deal with the strong feelings -- and impulses -- that come up in the course of family life. In PARENTS FORUM, we develop our emotional awareness with exercises using both active and passive communications skills: we practice expressing our own feelings and practice listening attentively to others express theirs.

Suppose that the two mothers described at the beginning of this chapter could, later, share with each other their disappointment in themselves at their angry and sarcastic outbursts. They could recall, too, the many caring and considerate moments they've had with their children. Maybe each could find a reasonably unstressed time to talk with her kids, to apologize and to ask for suggestions on how, as a family, they could avoid such blowups. Maybe these two moms could discuss the conflicts they each anticipate and agree to speak again afterwards, using the "bookend" technique described in Chapter 5.

When parents own up to their mistakes, they model this behavior for their children. Apologizing is a crucial step in improving family communication. However, an apology alone may be insufficient. A parent screams, apologizes, screams, apologizes. A teen breaks curfew, apologizes, breaks curfew again, and so on. An automatic or "pro forma" apology, one made without reflecting on the circumstances or motives leading up to the event that prompted it, may simply be a stepping stone in a circular path leading back to hurting a loved one again. You may notice such a pattern in your home. If you do, you can discuss that pattern and consider how to change it. Both participants may see changes they can make. Most of the time, it does "take two to tangle."

In a workshop, when parents describe an argument or
confrontation, we find it helpful to recall the agenda
questions four and five, about values and rules. How
do your values determine the household rules regarding parents speaking with each other? Does my behavior (yelling, name-calling, swearing) violate those
rules? Are rules for parent-to-parent discussion and
conflict the same as those for parent-to-child and
child-to-parent conversation and argument?

Are certain words not permitted? What sorts of expression are allowed, encouraged or forbidden when feelings run high? Are children encouraged to cry if they
feel like it? What about adults? Can we cry too? Who
sulks and for how long, usually? Are there time limits
for arguments and silences, for discussing and not discussing problems? What do you say and what helps
you "watch your words"? How do you know if you are
really listening or being listened to? Do you turn off
the radio, the television, the computer so that you can
hear and be heard?

As difficult as it is to do everything we need to do in
a day, it is sometimes even harder, at home, to take
time to be kind and to make time to listen. We want
to "let our hair down" and be able to let our defenses
down. But this can be dangerous in a stressful situation. The latitude we both need and expect at home
can lead to hurtful lapses in the way we speak to people we live with.

Don't family members deserve the same courtesy we
show to people outside our homes? Don't relatives and
friends deserve from us the kind of attention we'd like
to receive from them? Still, most of us have moments
when it is hard to resist the temptation to "come home
and kick the dog" to relieve frustrations we've experienced during the workday. Our goal in PARENTS FORUM

is to develop practices of diffusing tensions before they get the better of us, or rather, before they bring out the worst in us! We can teach our kids appropriate ways to deal with their frustrations by not giving them a "dog-kicking" role model. This is much easier to do if we take time to put some guidelines in place.

Family rules can spell out some ways to deal with these difficulties. For example, maybe a few minutes of quiet time after coming in the door will help each of us make a "gentle landing" after a busy day. If you find yourself "facing off" with your cranky five-year-old or your exhausted spouse, take a deep breath, listen as attentively as you can and then use words that you would like to hear if you were in your child's or partner's place: "What's the matter?" "Shall I just listen?" "Is there something I can do to help?" However, if you can't give them good attention, be honest about that: "This isn't a good time, could we talk later?" Be specific and then keep your promise. Perhaps set the timer for a brief period -- this might be a good tactic with a preschooler. You could say "Dad (or Mom) needs a time out." Or, for a larger issue or a longer delay, write a note and put it on the refrigerator, or give your spouse or child an IOU for listening.

Of course, when feelings run high they demand attention. My anger or my angry kid cannot be "shelved" indefinitely. Many cultures, including our own in North America, lack adequate support for expressing powerful negative feelings in a way that doesn't harm others. PARENTS FORUM is one of a number of programs striving to remedy this lack. It is true that expressing feelings at the wrong times, or in the wrong ways, can damage our relationships with people we care about. But emotions fuel our behaviors and failing to take time to recognize and channel or express them can do serious damage to our own and others' well-being. If we put thought in the driver's seat, even strong negative feelings can be expressed ways that minimize harm. Change is possible, although it does take practice and time to develop new patterns of behavior. We can learn to advocate for our own emotional needs and teach our children to do the same.

Speaking sharply to children is one thing. Sometimes you have to raise your voice to get their attention. Or if you have been yelling a lot, lower your voice. A change, in and of itself, will get attention. Choose your words carefully and try using the conversational formula: "I feel extremely frustrated and upset about your leaving the living room a mess because we're having company soon and I want this place to look nice!" Raising your voice in this instance can produce a desired result without causing harm. Shaming or humiliating words, on the other hand ("What the 'bleep' is the matter with you kids? You left this place a pigsty!"), whether they are spoken quietly or hurled full force, can be as damaging to both parties as a physical blow.

The rhyme, "Sticks and stones may break my bones, but words will never hurt me" might more accurately read, "Sticks and stones can break my bones and words can break my spirit." If the conversational climate in your home is more often stormy than sunny,

There was one moment when I knew I had made significant progress in becoming a calmer, more reasonable and more effective parent. Michael, my youngest, was five or six years old. His brother Luke, a teenager, had committed some misdeed. Michael, seeing my evident anger, advised me, "Mom, you'll have to speak sharply to Luke." If speaking sharply was the ultimate sanction, I had really made progress!

if you or your kids are yelling a lot, and you would like to change this, you can. Just as walking every day gradually tones your body, working daily to raise your emotional awareness can increase your peace of mind and harmony in your 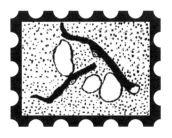 household. The changes need not be sudden and probably can't be. But they can be steady.

As I became aware of the damage that blaming and shaming language caused, I vowed to make changes in how I spoke to my boys. It was so difficult that I felt I was practically learning a new language. A key element in my re-education was the acceptance and support I received from other parents. They gently encouraged me to be honest about what had gone on and what was still going on in my family and loved me anyway, even though a lot of it wasn't pretty. Their gentleness with me helped me become more gentle with myself.

Gradually I developed more patience with my children. While I tried to be more honest with myself and with them about my feelings, I tried just as hard to consider their feelings and possible reactions. Our household

I write this as a parent, happy now to have peaceful relations, for the most part, with my grown sons. Let me share a young person's perspective. A friend of mine, a young woman about thirty years old, still suffers from her mother's unrelenting criticism. My friend said she finds it difficult to visit her family home, because everyone is so negative. She said she recently realized that, as a child, "I thought my mother hated me because she was so hateful to me."

> *In one intense parent weekend in the treatment program, the counselor leading the session asked each parent in the group to stand, in turn, and describe an incident where we had behaved in a way we later regretted. When my turn came, I remember crying as I described a time when I had hit one of my boys with uncontrolled anger. I remember the loving attention of the group and the parents sitting next to me holding my hands as I spoke. Saying out loud how I had hurt my son relieved the hurt -- from that incident and others -- hurt I had been holding inside. At that moment their warmth and understanding allowed me to forgive myself and I realized I could change.*

rules, posted on the refrigerator, began with a few lines about our values (a family "mission statement" you could call it) and continued with a list of do's and don'ts in various categories. Consequences for not following the rules (one particularly dreaded punishment was "no grilled cheese sandwiches") were spelled out too. The rules have been through many revisions, starting out short, getting longer and then shorter again once my boys moved out. Nearly fifteen years later, our rules are still posted. Learning to be both patient and honest is a challenge and, even with clear rules in plain sight, it is easy to get sidetracked. It takes time but we all can change.

Another technique that can be helpful is keeping a personal journal. I still find this a useful discipline when I face some difficult situation because it gives me a clear starting point for my efforts to change. Try keeping a journal or a brief log for a few days or a week to monitor the verbal "weather" in your home.

Each evening, for several days at least, take ten or fifteen minutes to write down one or two significant exchanges that took place during the day. You can do this writing exercise alone or, if your spouse or partner is willing, you can do it with him or her or with another family member. Consider how adults and children in your family speak to each other. The observation and comment should be gentle, of course, otherwise the cure could be worse than the complaint. Notice whether you repeatedly make light of each other's concerns. Do you try to convince family members that they don't really feel what they say they feel? Do you ignore each other? When one family member asks for support does another ask for the same, a kind of "one-up" game? Do people change the subject or interrupt each other frequently? Notes, if you take them, are best used to promote discussion and resolution of conflicts. Using them to support attacks and accusations defeats the purpose.

If writing seems too formal, or if a family member is unwilling to join you in this evaluation, you could make a telephone appointment with a friend and complete the exercise, over a few days' time, in conversation. Another person's perspective may be helpful. Referring to the questions from the PARENTS FORUM agenda may put your conversations (or arguments) in a clearer light as you consider, "Was that a Question 2 issue, about concern?" "...a Question 4 issue, about values?" "...a Question 7 issue, about saying goodbye?"

Perspectives differ, of course: I might feel terribly regretful at having lost my temper or terribly hurt at something my husband or son said. But after talking with him I might find, to my surprise, that he remembered neither incident!

A helpful reference is *The Verbally Abusive Relationship*, by Patricia Evans. It suggests patterns of speech that signal possible abusiveness and lists behaviors that go beyond simple yelling, such as withholding praise or accidentally-on-purpose "forgetting" about a promise to take a child to the movies, for example. Rather than worry excessively about real or imagined verbal abuse I suffered or inflicted, I now try to consider any hurtful exchange of words and talk it over with a friend. Whether my words hurt someone else or their words hurt me, it helps to talk about what happened with a third party. Identifying a problem is the first step toward remedying it. Try not to be too hard on yourself or family members. One incident of discounting a child's pain or one broken promise of a trip to the park does not establish a pattern. What counts is the over-all consistent emotional climate of our family lives.

Even in giving care, we can unthinkingly disrespect a child's feelings. A four-year-old falls, scrapes his knee and comes crying into the kitchen. Mom says, "Oh, don't be silly, what are you crying about? Don't make such a fuss over a little scrape!" She didn't hit him. She cleaned and bandaged his knee. But she also trivialized his feelings. As an isolated incident, such an exchange may not qualify as abuse. Repeated over time, however, such comments could set a child up to discount his or her own feelings as well as the feelings of playmates. If we consistently minimize our children's sadness, hurt or fear, they learn that these feelings are not important to us. A child then, perhaps deliberately or uncon-sciously, suppresses his feelings and in the process

> *Well-intentioned parents -- I count myself one -- can discourage a child. A sixth-grader's report card has A's in four subjects and a C in history. Instead of a big smile and, "I see you really worked hard this term!" Mom or Dad says, "What happened with your history grade?" One of my sons told me that he hated my saying, "Good effort!" because he heard it as, "You made a good effort but you came up short." I'm glad he told me. I stopped saying that.*

becomes less able to empathize with others.

In popular magazines, I've read several articles on the topic of bullying that say children may provoke in others the feelings they are discouraged from expressing themselves. For example, a child who is not allowed to show he is afraid, or who is ridiculed for showing fear, might try to intimidate other children. In trying to get our children to be "strong" or "tough" when physically or emotionally hurt -- before they're done experiencing and expressing their pain or disappointment -- we may be setting a pattern of disrespect for other people's feelings.

Watching our words and silences is not something many of us do naturally. But if we devote time to helping our children develop patience and understanding, just as we do to teaching them how to read and count, to identify colors and to ride a bike, they will acquire these qualities.

Apologizing doesn't come easily for many of us. It can be difficult, even uncomfortable, to say, "I'm sorry,"

especially if the phrase has not been part of your vocabulary in the past. One of the lessons of recovery that I find especially useful at times I've made mistakes is to keep my apology "brief, blunt and to the point." I try to say just one thing, "sorry," perhaps using, "I feel sorry about... because...," without looking back and justifying my mistake or looking forward and anticipating the other person's response. If the situation is one that has happened before or that is likely to recur, I may, as a reminder to myself as much as a signal to the other person, state a change I will make. Still, simpler is usually better.

Apologizing means taking a risk. The person receiving

> *At a class reunion not long ago, I met a high school friend and her husband and, as is common at such gatherings, we shared parenting "war stories." One of these offers a unique safety-valve tactic. Judy and Jack Palmer described how they would sit on the floor in a circle with their daughter and her preschool friends (the friends' parents too, sometimes), everyone with a pillow in their lap. Each person had a chance to tell the others what they were mad about and why. A kid, hitting her pillow, might say, "Take that, Mom, on the lips, for calling me a dope!" Mom would respond by holding her hands to her mouth and yelling, "Owwwww, that hurts!" Around the circle, Dad, hitting the pillow in his lap, might*

the apology may interpret the expression of regret as an opening for an attack. It is helpful if family rules are clear on how apologies are made and accepted. Apology, like praise, is best when it's genuine, unforced and focused. If I've screamed at my child, I could say, "I'm sorry for yelling and I see you look upset. I am completely out of patience. I feel very frustrated because you still haven't put away your building blocks!" Then take a breath, and consider next steps, both words and action.

As parents, we can make an effort to become conscious of the quality of our speaking and our listening right from the beginning. The concern here is not about an occasional tantrum or argument, but the overall day-in and day-out emotional and conversational climate in your home. Judgment about the seriousness of distress is yours to make. Reasonable people disagree, usually with a degree of calm. Unreasonable people disagreetoo, usually unreasonably. The trick, worth learning, is how to talk calmly about provocative issues and behaviors. It can be done.

Is your family's conversational style generally dismis-

say, "Take that, Jamie, on the hand, for knocking over the milk!" and Jamie would squeeze his hands together, crying out loud, "Ouuuuuch!" Mom's accusation, "Take that, Nancy, on the ear, for not listening to me about hanging up your clothes!" would provoke an, "Oh no, my ear, that hurts too much!" from Nancy. The game was a big success with neighborhood children who would come over and ask to play. I should emphasize that this game is not about trivializing physical abuse. Done in the right spirit, it can effectively relieve tension. As Judy and Jack described the game, feelings were heard, no one was hit, and the honesty and laughter of "Take That!" refreshed everyone.

sive? Is it manipulative? Is it competitive -- speakers not acknowledging each other, or trying to dominate each other? Or is it even combative -- with frequent or long-running arguments? If you recognize these patterns, do you want to change them? If impatience or disrespect is chronic and ingrained in one or more family members, it is unlikely that family harmony will burst out, like sun from behind the clouds, overnight. If one person makes a change, however small, other family members will sooner or later respond to that change. The person who wants to initiate a positive change may benefit from focused self-help programs and/or from professional counseling. If there are questions about the mental health or physical safety of a family member, obviously, seek help without delay. At the very least, seek advice about getting help.

If reading this chapter has made you uncomfortable, take the discomfort as a caution light, and slow down. The next time you feel angry, tired or sad, remember to breathe. Call someone, or sit down with someone, and talk about, cry about, laugh about whatever is upsetting you. Let your anger, fatigue and sadness out. Conversation with another parent can be a safety valve when your life feels like a pressure cooker.

Raising Parents

Chapter Seven

Children make their needs clear, "Feed me... love me... teach me... play with me... help me find my way in the world...." These needs recall the handy guide presented in Chapter Four and they do, in fact, persist into adulthood. As parents we want to meet our children's needs and we'll have a better chance of doing so if we acknowledge and address our own needs as well. In effect, parents need raising too! We need different kinds of support at different stages of our own and our children's development. Teen parents may need more help than a couple in their 20s or 30s. A first-time mother needs a different sort of assistance than a mother having her second or third baby. The challenge we sought to meet in founding PARENTS FORUM was to create an organization open enough and flexible enough for parents and others at all stages of life to give and get needed support for family life.

This chapter describes the steps we took in developing PARENTS FORUM in Cambridge and Somerville, Massachusetts. It also outlines our plan and practices, and suggests steps you can take to organize PARENTS FORUM in your community. Please see the note at the end regarding use of the PARENTS FORUM program and name.

In 1994, a couple of years after we organized our first PARENTS FORUM workshops, we learned that the United Nations had designated that year as the International Year of the Family. For us the timing could not have been better, as it offered a broader context for our efforts. The U.N. declaration read, in part, "Changes in our society [have] much affected and altered the family...[However] the family is a powerful agent for social, political, economic and cultural change and a potential vehicle for development. The family must be given assistance and -- if need be -- protection, so that it can fully assume its responsibilities as the basic unit of society."

These encouraging words helped us move forward. We realized that the struggles we faced were not unique and, more importantly, we saw that we could take action to "fully assume our responsibilities" as parents. From our own experiences we had learned the benefit of mutual support, but how could we get other parents involved?

Early on, we decided PARENTS FORUM events would be free to individuals so that there would be no monetary hurdle to participation. We felt that businesses, schools and other public and private agencies would support our activities through sponsorship and fees in order to foster healthy family life and create stronger communities. We chose to offer prizes as incentives for parents to come and to hold prize drawings both during and at the end of events to encourage parents to stay involved. We opted to keep monetary transactions of any sort out of our events. Fundraising would be separate from other activities.

We also decided that PARENTS FORUM would have no members. The question of membership came up in filing our articles of incorporation with the state. We chose to file as a non-membership organization, keeping an open-door policy, for two reasons: to avoid creating either a financial hurdle to participation, with members paying dues (and some not able to pay) or an emotional hurdle, with an in-group and an out-group. We call the people who take part in PARENTS FORUM events participants and the people who organize them coordinators.

Discussions in the first few years got stuck, several times, on the question of professional versus non-professional leadership. We eventually chose volunteers leaders because we believe our Tools of the Trade and Eight Questions offer an accessible and adaptable, low-tech curriculum that non-professionals can successfully use in leading group discussions. Along with eliminating financial and membership barriers, we avoid unsolicited "advice-giving" in the workshops. The reason for this is to blur, if not erase, the line between those giving help and those receiving it. A suggestion for solving a problem may be what someone needs, but he or she is more likely to accept it if they have asked for it. The suggestion may meet with less resistance, too, if it is presented as one option rather than the one "right answer." Workshop facilitators model empathetic listening and share their own struggles, before giving any advice. Often participants and facilitators tell each other about community resources and both benefit from the exchange.

We wanted volunteer workshop leaders -- our coordinators -- to act as facilitators, not experts, in order to

One of the coordinators of our first spin-off group described what she got from PARENTS FORUM when she volunteered to come to our community television station to be filmed for a public service announcement. I had no idea what she would say but I shouldn't have worried. "I learned," she said, "that the most important thing I can give my kids is creativity and I don't need to give them so much stuff." She described how she had gotten help cleaning and straightening her children's playroom, how she had called on other PARENTS FORUM participants to baby-sit occasionally and how she had organized a number of community events for other parents. She mentioned how she'd had fun, too, and how much it meant to her to be able to help others. She and her husband had developed their leadership skills and self-confidence to the point that they had agreed to co-chair their school's Parent Teacher Association.

honor parents' leadership in their families. Many counselors, mental health care providers and parenting education specialists recognize the value of mutual help as
prevention or as follow-up to professional help. They
and others encouraged our efforts. Still, we had a lot to
do when we began "raising" our program, as the idea of
positive mutual support for parents was new. We had
to promote and develop our program at the same time.
Here, in outline form, are the elements needed to create
PARENTS FORUM in your community:

- people to organize the activities and to seek
  community involvement from others: coordina-
  tor(s), workshop facilitator(s), treasurer, writer
  or publicist, secretary and other volunteers

- people to participate: parents and others of all
  ages

- prizes for participants: goods and gift certificates for goods and services useful to families --
  this includes the basics (food and clothing) as
  well as museum passes, tickets to movie the-
  aters and sports events and vouchers for classes for children or adults and so on

- sponsors: librarians and literacy advocates,
  educators, public health agencies, business
  people, service clubs, artists, athletes and
  sports clubs, journalists (print, broadcast, and
  cable and electronic media), some to provide
  direct financial support and some to offer prizes

- agencies serving families in need as beneficiar-
  ies of the surplus goods donated in book and
  toy exchanges

- places to meet: library, cultural center, workplace, school, clinic, church or temple

107

- volunteers to provide childcare for meetings with appropriate cultural activities

- refreshments (remember, "Feed me!")

- and, last but not least, organized activities, including the workshops described in previous chapters as well as several other activities described below.

To begin, get a small group of people together and take an inventory of your needs and skills. What sorts of activities will you organize and when? Who is willing to take the lead? Who will come to your events and how will you contact and attract them? Who will ask for donations and keep track of expenditures? Who will call or visit prospective hosts and sponsors?

A note or two on fundraising is in order at this point, as asking for donations can be difficult for many people. The best I can say about fundraising is that as difficult as it may be at the outset, it gets easier each time you do it. When you approach a friend, associate or a business person for money, you are, of course, asking for something, but you are also offering something important in return. You are offering prospective donors a chance to make a difference in their community. If you use the skills you developed and practiced in Chapter Five, these conversations become easier. If the plan for your activity is clear, if the benefit to families in your community is evident and, most important, if you are convinced of its value, you are very likely to receive the donation or support you request. Of course, some people will still say NO, but they may be able to offer assistance another time or may give you valuable advice on other sources of support.

In addition to seeking donations, PARENTS FORUM requests fees for its services from host agencies. Our activities offer a natural choice for schools, religious congregations, clinics and other agencies seeking parent support activities. Established groups, like PTA, PTO or an on-going parent discussion group at a clinic, make natural hosts for PARENTS FORUM, as do family resource centers or work/life programs which are becoming more numerous with government, foundation and corporate sponsorship. Also, some companies have an individual or a committee responsible for the firm's community involvement. Such a company might want to send volunteers to help with a community Book and Toy Exchange. Our signature event, an exchange works well on its own or as a lead-in to a workshop.

A BOOK AND TOY EXCHANGE, with planning and publicity efforts usually beginning three months in advance, can take place in a library or other community center from 11:00 to 1:00 on a Saturday. The library or another agency donates the space and announces the event in its calendars. Volunteer coordinators send announcements to schools, home-schooling families, churches and newspapers and they solicit prizes and refreshments from local businesses. PARENTS FORUM reaches out to all segments of the community, including public, parochial and private school families as well as home-schoolers.

During the ten days before the announced date, people drop off their donations at branch libraries. Donations are also accepted on the day of the Book and Toy Exchange. We especially request books on parenting and family life and we ask local agencies to send literature about their programs for parents and families. Then it happens: Coordinators and volunteers who agreed to help come to the designated location and organize the donated items by age group. People come with their kids -- we have a table with art activities for the children -- and parents and children freely give and take the books and toys that have been set out. Door prizes are drawn mid-way through the exchange and at the end. A local charity -- a shelter or youth center, for example -- receives the books and toys remaining at the end of the two hours. In choosing a homeless shelter, for example, as the beneficiary of a Book and Toy Exchange, PARENTS FORUM recognizes and responds to peoples' desire to help others who are experiencing greater need.

At the PARENTS FORUM Book & Toy Exchange in October 2000 at the Cambridge (Mass.) Public Library, Susana, from Argentina and Cambridge, mother of Markie, age 2 1/2, said, "Great job! Do it again!" Igor, a World Boston Community Connections visitor from Vyborg, near St. Petersburg, and the father of Slavik, six years old, commented, "We have nothing like this in Russia. So many people, everyone is so interested, and everybody needs it, this bring and take." "Fantastic! I saw the flyer in the library . . . I couldn't resist. I have a big bag of books and I'm still looking," added Ceane,

Volunteers at the event screen the donations, sort them and keep the tables in order during the two-hour exchange. Book and Toy Exchanges offer a respite from the materialism and commercialism that seem to have ever greater sway in our society. For two hours people give what they can and take what they need without money changing hands. Parents have a chance to teach their children about charity, "We'll give away this book you no longer enjoy. What would you like to take? [and] Leave some things for others to take, too." The exchange of books and toys mirrors the exchange of insights and experiences that takes place in our conversations. Parents make new friends at these events and are able to pick up brochures about local resources for families.

Another successful PARENTS FORUM activity, PLAY-ROOM MAKEOVERS, grew out of an informal planning meeting when the hosting parent, acknowledging the clutter of toys, admitted, "I went overboard last Christmas." We made an appointment for a two-hour session one evening and together sorted through puzzles, trucks, dolls and blocks. Some items were clearly ready to be discarded or given away. Others were set aside for when their children were a little older. We

mother of Zoe, 2 1/2 years old, from Charlestown. At the end of the two-hour free event more than a dozen bags of books and toys remained for the beneficiary of the event, a family shelter in Boston for people recovering from alcohol and other drug abuse. Door prizes included gift certificates from restaurants and career consultants. Like the other Book and Toy Exchanges held in Cambridge and Somerville, once or twice a year, this one elicited favorable comments from a social worker and therapist who attended, "Parents need this and it would be great if you offer regular groups."

designated a place for every kind of toy. The result was a clean playroom and, while it may not have stayed that way for long, the order we created was uplifting for both parents and kids. It served as a reference point and an inspiration for regular playroom cleaning and cleaning out. It gave us an opportunity to socialize while doing something useful. This activity illustrates, too, the way PARENTS FORUM coordinators can develop new ideas on their own.

Two mini-workshops have evolved through participation in community events organized by other agencies. The first is TELLING OUR OWN STORIES, where we set up a display table with our program literature at a fair or other community event. We engage parents, with their children, in conversation, asking them to reminisce about happy family events -- basically answering the first agenda question "What do you like about your family?" This mini-workshop can serve as volunteer training, with individual volunteers serving for an hour at the table to get experience talking informally with new people, without the pressure of standing up in front of a group. This activity can be

At Family Fun Day, an annual Cambridge Family Literacy Collaborative event, we once invited parents and children to cut out a hand shape and write on it the name of their favorite book, adding each favorite book to a poster as the day went along. Another year we invited fair-goers to talk about their family experiences. An elder volunteering at the event told a story about her many years as a foster parent, proudly emphasizing that all the children who came to her finished high school. People love to share their stories and have too few opportunities to do so.

done, too, as an art activity for children alone, or while parents are involved in workshop discussions. I still have the drawings on poster board that children created at our first poster-making session at the Cambridge Public Library, delightful illustrations of birthday parties, walks in the park and families playing games together.

Another mini-workshop, based on our third agenda question, is called HOW TO TELL SOMEBODY SOMETHING THEY'D RATHER NOT HEAR (HTTSSTRNH), and was developed as part of Charm School at the Massachusetts Institute of Technology. This event, a four-hour "manners fair," is presented on the MIT campus each January. You might be surprised at a science and engineering university venturing into the etiquette business, but the event is a great success and has gotten national media coverage. There are booths on table manners and how to make introductions, demonstrations of ballroom dancing, "elevator etiquette," role-plays on asking for a date, library manners, presentations on telephone manners, effective e-mail and how to write social correspondence (sympathy notes, thank-you notes and invitations) and, recently added, a session on sorting laundry.

At the PARENTS FORUM booth, HTTSSTRNH, volunteer faculty-for-a-day discuss troublesome situations described by people who join us for a five-or ten-minute session. We cover a variety of sticky situations: firing somebody or quitting a job, telling a student s/he didn't pass an exam, breaking up with a boyfriend or girlfriend, confronting somebody about their heavy drinking. Even minor mini-confrontations, like re-claiming one's place in line if someone has cut in front of you, come up. Following the PARENTS FORUM protocol, we do brief role-plays using the conversational formula "I feel... about... because...."

113

The groups are small, usually ten or twelve people and role-play participants leave with new strategies and energy for addressing challenging situations in their personal and academic lives. Those who do not take part in a role-play still learn a useful lesson when they see that sticky situations -- and life is full of them -- can be more successfully handled if uncomfortable feelings are addressed.

Workshops, book and toy exchanges, playroom makeovers, and the mini-workshops "Telling Our Own Stories" and HTTSSTRNH are the basic program elements of PARENTS FORUM. Each helps in one or more ways to support us as we strive to meet the enormous demands of family and society. We try, throughout our activities, to keep in perspective those demands and our own sometimes unreasonable expectations. Wherever we live, we have similar hopes for our children. We also need similar kinds of support if we are to provide for their well-being and healthy development.

At PARENTS FORUM, we believe that there are a few general requirements for a successful program for "raising parents." Programs must be free, frequent and fun, must solicit parents' feedback and must serve refreshments. We call these "the five F's." We also ask workshops hosts to provide childcare, as the cost of a baby-sitter or the inconvenience of leaving a child at home can discourage parents from attending. If you are interested in creating your own PARENTS FORUM, it is important also to consider the "five W's" of parenting education:

WHAT is parenting education? Practical skills coupled with knowledge about child and adolescent development.

WHO offers parenting education? Many people in par-

ents' lives teach us, or can teach us, important lessons, among them medical and mental health care
providers and ordinary folks including our own parents, friends and neighbors. WHO pays? Public and
private agencies and community-minded businesses;
parents themselves may also pay for courses or
professionally led seminars.

WHERE does parenting education happen? Lots of
places, from formal settings like classrooms to informal ones like the bleachers at a ball game.

WHEN does it happen? Not often enough! Kindergarten
was once an innovation. Now it's part of almost all
school programs. We want to put parents' concerns
on the policy agenda of government, business, and
civil society and we see universally accessible parenting education as our long-term goal.

WHY is parenting education important? The cost of
parents being ill-prepared to raise children is borne
by all of us, personally and socially.

How can we better prepare to feed... love... teach...
play with... and help our children find their way in the
world? We need to take time to prepare, but how can
we find the time when so many of our daily tasks are
not optional? A crying baby needs to be fed, changed,
or soothed. Toddlers need to be picked up or dropped
off at daycare. Preschoolers need an art activity or a
trip to the park. A school-age child needs a hug, or
homework checked, or a story read. A teen or young
adult child needs advice (seldom), needs a ride somewhere (often) or needs money (still more often!) A
supervisor insists on a report or a customer needs an
order by the end of the day. An appliance signals (the
microwave beeps, the clothes dryer buzzes) calling our
attention. We are lucky to have them, of course - the

kids, the work and the conveniences -- but taking
breaks between those urgent tasks is as essential as
the tasks themselves. We also need food, friendship,
information and skills, fun times and a chance to
become involved in our community. PARENTS FORUM
and other programs for parents play an essential role
in community life. Businesses and community agencies can help by recognizing parenting education as
a cornerstone of family support.

The United Nations
International Year of the
Family, celebrated in
1994, had as its emblem
a heart enfolding a heart
under a roof and its
theme was "family is
the smallest democracy
at the heart of society."
In PARENTS FORUM,
we develop our ability to
resolve conflicts respect-
fully (if not always dem-
ocratically) and we focus on our capacity to give each
other and our children intelligent and caring attention.
We try to "dwell in a place of abundance" even under
constraints in material circumstances and under pressure of time. Parents, especially parents of young children, have too little of the latter. Giving our children
and each other good attention during the moments we
are able to spend together is a priceless gift.

IMPORTANT NOTE:

PARENTS FORUM has applied for trademark registration for our services. We welcome inquiries from parents and other interested in starting their own groups and charge a modest fee for using our name and program plan. Income from the sale of this book and from licensing fees will fund administrative support for our organization and translation of our materials into other languages. We have had inquiries from parents and parenting education volunteers and professionals in countries as near as Canada and Mexico and as far away as Ukraine, Pakistan and Zambia. Let us hear from you.

Love and Order

Chapter Eight

A year or so ago a couple involved in PARENTS FORUM invited me over for a visit. We were sitting at the kitchen table when their almost six-year-old son sidled up to his mother. As he climbed into her lap, she said, "Why don't we ask Eve that question you asked me earlier?" and, with some encouragement, he asked, "Why are there big people who are mean?"

His mother told me she'd replied, "There are more good people than bad people in the world, but there still are some just plain mean folks." She was right, of course. The world is imperfect and people are imperfect. The underlying question I heard in her son's words, however, was, "How do people get to be mean?"

So, to my friend's response I added that I thought big people who are mean probably had parents who were mean to them when they were little. As we talked, I wondered aloud what those mean parents did and didn't do. It occurred to me that they probably punished their children harshly and probably weren't very loving. I recalled the PARENTS FORUM workshop lesson on thoughts and feelings. In that lesson we considered our behavior from the perspective of thoughts and how we keep order in our households, and from the perspective of feelings and how we express affection. Mean parents may establish too little order (or enforce it too harshly) and may give too little love (or

Near the end of a long stay-at-home day when my boys were little, I recall one of them nagging me for more cookies. These happened to be lemon-flavored cookies. Frustrated, I yelled, "There have to be limits!" and, confusing lemons with limits he replied, "I want more limits!" If only kids were this clear all the time. They need our love, and cookies sometimes, but they need order too, and limits on the cookies.

show it inconsistently). Effective parents provide adequate measures of both order and love. Love and order. That sounds oh-so-simple, but giving our kids enough of both and achieving a balance between the two on a day-to-day, sometimes minute-to-minute basis, can be difficult indeed.

When we are new parents, our lives are completely taken up with the baby. As parents of school kids, then parents of young adults, we learn, little by little, to do less as our children learn to do more and more for themselves. Only by taking breaks now and then from the day-to-day work of raising children can we get the perspective we need on their progress and on our own.

> *Babies need immediate and nearly constant attention. A new father said, "There's no give and take. We give. He takes! It's total slavery." But he said this with a smile, knowing that as time passes there will be moments, and then longer and longer periods, when he can expect his son to wait. Just not now -- the baby is only six months old.*

How can we get the time to develop perspective? Our children always need our love, but they may want it expressed differently at different stages. Similarly, they need us to provide order in their lives in different ways at different ages. How can we judge whether we are doing a good job? To "keep tabs" on the balance of love and order in our parenting, we can benefit from reassurance, support, and information from other adults. The order of these three elements is important: first, emotional reassurance, then practical support, and, finally, objective information. If the information the other person offers -- in whatever guise, either advice or instruction -- comes first, it may create a logjam, only increasing the frustration a parent feels from lack of either reassurance or support or both.

Think back to the exercise on expressing concern in "Tools of the Trade" where you used the formula "I feel ... about ... because ..." Remember that the feeling word comes first. Saying how you feel can, sometimes almost literally, take a "load off your chest." Describing the situation that caused the feeling can be a relief too. Even better is getting help with the situation. (Note that, while PARENTS FORUM does not offer specific services, as participants get to know one another and become friends, they may help each other out with childcare, housework, finances and that all important referral: the name of a dependable plumber.) After dealing with these two elements, the feelings and the behavior, we can talk about the whys and wherefores, and get the information we need to understand the situation and the feelings it brought up. Keeping these three elements in order, especially the part about monitoring our own feelings, is essential to maintaining a good balance in parenting. Expressing our feelings (to an appropriate person,

When I was expecting my second baby, I recall another expectant mother showing up at my door doing a city-sponsored survey of families' needs. She and I discovered that our first-borns had almost the same birthday and that our new babies were due about the same time. We became friends almost overnight and remain so today, having traded childcare in those early, busy days and shared many concerns and many more joys over the years. We joke that our now-grown children will have to arrange for us to visit each other in our nursing homes just as we arranged their "play dates" when they were little.

at an appropriate time) opens the door to figuring out solutions to day-to-day challenges.

In parenting, unlike writing, there are no first drafts, no scribbling down a few trial words of mothering or fathering then pressing the delete key. Everything counts. "No back-talk, no recall," as my sons would yell upon claiming the preferred seat in the car. How many times have I heard words coming out of my mouth and known they were wrong? Too many to count. What do I do differently today, as a parent? I remember to breathe and I ask more questions, of myself and of my sons. I also talk often with other parents and listen to their insights, especially the unwelcome ones. The ability to accept criticism is a valuable trait to develop, one I am still working on. I sure wish I didn't encounter so many "teachable moments!"

While we work to strike that difficult balance in our own households, what is going on in our neighbors' homes and in the homes of our children's classmates? Do relatives and friends support us in setting rules and holding our kids responsible for following them? If they don't, we can ask for this support. When they do, we can say thanks. Do our communities offer us formal and informal support in meeting the many challenges of raising a family? If they don't, we can advocate for this support. When they do, we can share the experience: tell friends and neighbors and mention successful programs to others who can spread the word.

In 1956 my father, Richard Odiorne, wrote a book, *Why They Came*, for the centennial celebration of my home town, Yellow Springs, Ohio. His opening and closing words capture the spirit of community that I believe we all want for ourselves and our children wherever we happen to live. It is the spirit that PARENTS FORUM seeks to promote.

In the introduction, he stated the book's purpose as twofold: to present highlights of the town's history and to affirm, for present and future residents, the town's "essential qualities of neighborliness, eagerness for new ideas, and simplicity of life in a busy world." In the closing paragraphs, he describes Yellow Springs as "a town in which quality of work can be more important than quantity; where people do not need to be caught in a race for bigness; where neighborliness promotes tolerance and understanding."

As our communities have become bigger, as our lives are too often invaded by news of violence if not directly by threat of violence or violence itself, and as commercialism encroaches further into our communities and our lives, we can maintain a positive vision. We can try to create loving and orderly homes. We can strive to be neighborly and tolerant. We can maintain an eagerness for new ideas. We can "live simply," as the expression goes, "so that others may simply live." I believe that we can and must do all of these things. I hope that PARENTS FORUM will be a strong partner in the many personal, community and global efforts to do so.

RESOURCES

These resources (listed on page 186) are provided in the interest of improving support for parents, others caring for children, and parent groups, and in the interest of improving networking among parents and the organizations and professionals who serve us. The listings are for United States organizations, unless otherwise indicated, and many are in the Boston, Massachusetts area where PARENTS FORUM is located.

The list is intended as a starting point for you, your family or your parent group to find the support you need and the activities you want. Most listings are for non-commercial, non-academic programs that directly serve parents and for business organizations and service clubs that support community programming. We also list several Chambers of Commerce, as these often provide information about businesses, organizations and professionals serving parents. In addition to general listings, you will find several for education of the Deaf, literacy, mental health, substance abuse and suicide prevention.

Public and private agencies serving children, such as libraries, schools, after-school programs and community schools, museums, recreation centers and sports programs, as well as churches and temples, may also offer programs for parents. Some larger employers in the US have "work/life" programs and/or family resource centers that provide information and seminars on parenting. In many US cities and towns, there are parenting newspapers and newsletters with calendars of events for families and informative articles.

Also useful to parents, but not listed here, are education associations (NAEYC and NAEVYC, National Associations for the Education of the Young Child and ...the Very Young Child, for example), youth organizations (such as Boys & Girls Clubs, YMCA's, YWCA's and Family Y's, Girl Scouts / Boy Scouts, Big Brothers / Big Sisters), and elder services (like Grandparents and Foster Grandparents programs). Medical societies, notably the American Association of Pediatrics, have material and programs of interest to parents, as may unions, civic associations, and cultural and immigrant community organizations.

Organizations do not pay to be included in our list. The information was verified with the agency. We welcome inquiries from agencies about inclusion in our next edition. Readers, please send us comments on any agency you contact and names of organizations you would like to see in a next edition of this handbook. Because our location gives the list a geographical bias, we will especially appreciate contact information for parents associations, organizations serving families, and business and service clubs beyond the Boston area. Please tell us how the organization helped you or your parent group and send us all available information, including, if possible, when it was founded, its size and service area.

If there are no parenting programs in your area, perhaps you can find a sponsor and the support to get one going! We welcome your inquiries.

PARENTS FORUM
144 Pemberton Street
Cambridge MA 02140-2509
TEL: 617 - 864-3802
EMAIL: info@parentsforum.org
WEB: www.parentsforum.org

The ALGEBRA PROJECT, Inc.
99 Bishop Allen Drive
Cambridge MA 02139
TEL: 617 - 491-0200
FAX: 617 - 491-0499
EMAIL: apinc@algebra.org
-or-
Algebra Project Southern Initiative
c/o Positive Innovations
P.O. Box 20658
Jackson MS 39289
TEL: 601 - 969-3198
FAX: 601 - 969-3291
EMAIL: ddennissr@aol.com
WEB: www.algebraproject.org

Organized in 1982, The Algebra Project is a community-based middle-school (grade 6,7,8) program that aims to provide all students with the conceptual understanding of mathematics that will enable them to complete the college preparatory high school mathematics sequence. The project embraces the notion that mathematics literacy is necessary in a society where technology is rapidly transforming the skills required both for entry into the economic mainstream and for full and informed participation in political life. The program is being implemented at over twenty sites in 13 states in the South, the West Coast, the Midwest and the Northeast. Over 100 schools, serving more than 40,000 students, are involved in The Algebra Project. Many sites are set up in urban and rural areas to work specifically with African-American and Hispanic-American communities that are traditionally under-served. The Algebra Project conducts teacher training workshops and builds local networks of adults and youth who support and work to promote math literacy.

ALLIANCE FOR CHILDHOOD

P.O. Box 444
College Park MD 20741
TEL: 888 - 644-3272
FAX: 301 - 779-3272
EMAIL: info@allianceforchildhood.net
WEB: www.allianceforchildhood.org

The Alliance for Childhood was founded in 1999 during a series of meetings in New York (U.S.) London (U.K.) and Stuttgart (Germany). It is a growing partnership of parents, teachers, medical professionals, researchers, child advocates and others who are deeply concerned about the growing stress in children and their declining health and well-being. Through publications, conferences, and focused projects the Alliance seeks to address the underlying causes of the problems and inspire change. Alliance chapters are opening up in North American cities as well as around the world, including Mexico, Argentina, Brazil, Thailand and a number of countries in eastern and western Europe.

AMERICAN TOY INSTITUTE (ATI)

1115 Broadway, Suite 400
New York NY 10010
TEL: 212 - 675-1141

ATI is the educational and charitable affiliate of the Toy Manufacturers of America, Inc. (TMA), a trade association for U.S. producers and importers of toys and holiday decorations founded in 1916. The organization publishes a series of pamphlets covering toy selection and play, including a guide to toys for children who are blind or visually impaired.

ANPAF / ASSOCIAÇION NACIONAL DE PADRES DE FAMILIA

Av. Pacífico 151, Col. El Rosedal
C.P. 04330 México D.F. México
TEL: (52) 5 - 689-7102
FAX: (52) 5 - 689-7038
EMAIL: anpafjgp@netmex.com
WEB: orbita.starmedia.com/~anpaf

ANPAF's primary goal is to encourage parents to participate actively in their children's education. It originated as a Federal District parents association in 1933 and in 1980 was designated a national association under a general education act. ANPAF includes over 172,000 school associations, 829 municipal associations, 84 regional associations and 30 state associations, representing 18 million parents throughout Mexico. In addition to its support for basic education, ANPAF also promotes school health programs, parent training and voter registration and constantly seeks to improve the services provided to parents.

THE ASPIRA ASSOCIATION
Parent Leadership Programs

1444 Eye Street NW, Suite 800
Washington DC 20005
TEL: 202 - 835-3600
FAX: 202 - 835-3613
EMAIL: info@aspira.org
WEB: www.aspira.org

ASPIRA serves Puerto Rican and other Latino youth and their families through leadership development and education. The organization was founded in 1961 to address the exceedingly high drop-out rate and low educational attainment of Puerto Rican youth in New York City. It has become a national association with statewide associate organizations in Connecticut, Florida, Illinois, New Jersey, New York, Pennsylvania and Puerto Rico. While still mainly a Puerto Rican organization, it now reaches out to include all Latinos and a significant group of non-Latinos throughout the United States. Presently, ASPIRA serves over 25,000 students each year in over 400 schools, through its core activity, the ASPIRA Clubs.

AT-HOME DAD
61 Brightwood Avenue
North Andover MA 01845-1702
TEL: 978 - 685-7931
EMAIL: athomedad@aol.com
WEB: www.athomedad.com

Founded in 1994, AtHomeDad is an organization of about 1,000 members serving as a peer support group for fathers who choose to stay at home and raise their children as well as for fathers who are heads of single-family households. The *At-Home Dad* quarterly newsletter, with subscribers in 45 states, lists members of the national network of at-home dads. It also includes personal stories and offers advice on a variety of topics including playgroups and home businesses. AtHomeDad sponsors a convention in Chicago each November.

BECAUSE I LOVE YOU (B.I.L.Y.)
P.O. Box 473
Santa Monica CA 90406-0473
TEL: 310 - 659-5289 or
          818 - 882-4881
FAX: 323 - 585-4762
EMAIL: bily1982@aol.com
WEB: www.becauseiloveyou.org

131

B.I.L.Y. is a Los Angeles-based non-profit national organization founded in 1982 to support parents of troubled children of any age. It promotes structure, consequences and consistency in raising kids. Meetings are led by parents and are designed to help parents who have children with behavioral attitude problems, physical and/or verbal abuse, substance abuse, irregular school attendance/poor grades, runaway situations and other forms of defiance of authority. In addition to weekly parent group meetings, BILY offers a once-a-year communication camp for parents and family members. BILY has helped more than 90,000 people regain control of their lives and improve the quality of communication within their families.

BEFRIENDERS INTERNATIONAL
26 Elysium Gate
126 New Kings Road
London SW6 4LZ UK
TEL: (44) 731-0101
FAX: (44) 731-8008
EMAIL: admin@befrienders.org
WEB: www.befrienders.org

Befrienders International is dedicated to establishing effective suicide prevention services worldwide staffed by volunteers. Founded in 1974, twenty-one years after the founding of The Samaritans in the United Kingdom, Befrienders International has a unique role to develop volunteer-staffed suicide prevention services worldwide. The need for such services is shown by the estimated one million suicides which occur each year and the four million contacts made to Befrienders International centers by people in emotional crisis and at risk of suicide. In over 40 countries, over 350 autonomous centers affiliated with

Befrienders International provide confidential listening and befriending services for the suicidal and those in emotional crisis. Many centers and national associations have adopted the name, Befrienders, others have names with similar meanings in the local language. Many continue to use Samaritans.

BUSINESS FOR SOCIAL RESPONSIBILITY
609 Mission Street, 2nd Floor
San Francisco CA 94105-3506
TEL: 415 - 537-0890
FAX: 415 - 537-0889
WEB: www.bsr.org

Business for Social Responsibility (BSR) is a membership organization for companies of all sizes and sectors. BSR's mission is to be the leading global resource providing members with innovative products and services that help companies be commercially successful in ways that demonstrate respect for ethical values, people, communities and the environment.

CAMBRIDGE FAMILY LITERACY COLLABORATIVE
159 Thorndike Street
Cambridge MA 02141
TEL: 617 - 349-6263
FAX: 617 - 349-6415
EMAIL: cambridgereads@hotmail.com

Founded in 1998, the Cambridge Family Literacy Collaborative (CFLC) is a partnership of staff from City of Cambridge Public Schools, Libraries, and Department of Human Services; the Cambridge Health Alliance and other public agencies; along with staff and volunteers from nonprofit organizations who pool their time, energy and resources to educate the community about family literacy and encourage a citywide commitment to family literacy. Family Literacy is an educational model which focuses on the strengths and needs of the family and recognizes parents as children's first teachers. The collaborative organizes a Family Fun Day in celebration of National Family Literacy Month in November, conducts a public information campaign about family literacy, and offers networking opportunities for practitioners and others involved in early childhood and adult education, parenting education, and literacy efforts.

CAMBRIDGE SENIOR VOLUNTEER CLEARINGHOUSE

56 Brattle Street
P.O. Box 9113
Cambridge MA 02238
TEL: 617 - 864-6688
FAX: 617 - 497-7532
EMAIL: senvol@igc.org

Founded in 1994, the Clearinghouse matches adults age 55 or older interested in volunteering with Cambridge agencies that can use their skills and talents. The program works with non-profit and public sector agencies to identify opportunities for mature volunteers and supports the efforts of volunteer managers to recruit, train and successfully utilize mature volunteers. It also maintains and distributes a list of Cambridge-based organizations that involve mature volunteers in their programs.

CHAMBER OF COMMERCE of Cambridge

859 Massachusetts Avenue
Cambridge MA 02139
TEL: 617 - 876-4100

FAX: 617 - 354-9874
EMAIL: ccinfo@cambcc.org
WEB: www.cambridgechamber.org

Through special events, seminars and publications, the Chamber promotes networking among members and keeps them informed about new developments and issues affecting their businesses. The Chamber also provides information to prospective residents. Through committee work and community activism, Chamber members play a vital role in making Cambridge a better place to live, do business, visit, work and study.

CHAMBER OF COMMERCE of Somerville
2 Alpine Street
P.O. Box 343
Somerville MA 02144
TEL: 617 - 776-4100
FAX: 617 - 776-1157
EMAIL: info@somervillema.org
WEB: www.somervillema.org

The Somerville Chamber of Commerce serves as a vehicle for business networking and a voice in local public affairs. Neighborhood-based and industry-based interest groups help members expand their relationships and influence within the community. Residents and visitors alike enjoy a wide variety of entertainment activities including Magic Circle Children's Theater (at Tufts University) and Artbeat, a daylong festival held each summer.

CHARACTER COUNTS!sm
Josephson Institute of Ethics
4640 Admiralty Way, Suite 1001
Marina del Rey CA 90292-6610

TEL: 310 - 306-1868
FAX: 310 - 827-1864
EMAIL: CC@JIethics.org
WEB: www.charactercounts.org

The CHARACTER COUNTS!sm Coalition seeks to
fortify the lives of America's young people with
consensus ethical values called the "Six Pillars of
Character." These values, which transcend divisions
of race, creed, politics, gender and wealth, are: trust-
worthiness, respect, responsibility, fairness, caring
and citizenship. The Coalition both builds awareness
of these consensus values and teaches them to the
young in support of the paramount role of parents.
The program came out of The Aspen Declaration in
1992 and efforts to find a common ground for character education. The program is a voluntary non-
governmental citizen action initiative with over fifty
national and regional member organizations and
individual volunteers in local communities.

CHILD GROUP THERAPY ASSOCIATION
P.O. Box 521
Watertown MA 02472
TEL: 617 - 796-0150
EMAIL: sravagni@partners.org
WEB: www.cgta.net

The Children's Group Therapy Association (CGTA)
as established in 1968 by a group of professionals
who are actively involved in the field of children's
group therapy. The association functions as a support system for group therapists and as an advocate
for quality group services for children, adolescents
and parents. The Association presents an annual
conference in May and provides training opportunities and informational services to practitioners.

Membership in CGTA is open to professionals invested in children's and adolescent group therapy who have an interest in facilitating the expansion of training opportunities in the field.

CHILDREN'S DEFENSE FUND
25 E. Street NW
Washington DC 20001
TEL: 202 - 628-8787
FAX: 202 - 662-3520
EMAIL: cdfinfo@childrensdefense.org
WEB: www.childrensdefense.org

The mission of the Children's Defense Fund is to "Leave No Child Behind" and to ensure every child a healthy start, a head start, a fair start, a safe start and a moral start in life and successful passage to adulthood with the help of caring families and communities.

CHILDREN'S TRUST FUND
294 Washington Street, Suite 640
Boston MA 02108
TEL: 617 - 727-8957
TEL: 888 - 775-4543 (toll-free in
              Massachusetts, outside Boston area)
FAX: 617 - 727-8997

Founded in 1988, the Children's Trust Fund leads statewide efforts (in Massachusetts) to support parents and strengthen families thereby preventing child abuse. As an umbrella organization, it funds, evaluates and promotes the work of over one hundred agencies that serve parents. The Children's Trust Fund's three main goals are to:

• ensure that all families in Massachusetts
  have access to community-based family sup-

137

port services, including parenting education and newborn home visiting,

- ensure that every elementary school child and preschooler has access to training and practice in important personal safety skills that can help protect them from abuse and abduction,

- raise public awareness and influence public policy about the importance of child abuse prevention.

CONFEDERACION INTERNACIONAL DE APOYO FAMILIAR / CIAF
See FAAF

CIVICUS
World Alliance for Citizen Participation
919 18th Street NW, 3rd Floor
Washington DC 20006
TEL: 202 - 331-8518
FAX: 202 - 331-8774
EMAIL: info@civicus.org
WEB: www.civicus.org

CIVICUS, a membership organization open to institutions and individuals, is dedicated to promoting a worldwide community of informed, inspired, committed citizens who are actively engaged in confronting the challenges facing humanity. It publishes a week-

ly online bulletin featuring key trends and emerging issues in civil society and organizes a world assembly on these topics every two years. Next world assembly will be held in Vancouver, Canada in August 2001.

COLLABORATIVE CENTER FOR CHILD WELL-BEING

750 Commerce Drive, Suite 400
Atlanta GA 30030
TEL: 404 - 592-1400
          and tollfree 800 - 765-7349
FAX: 404 - 371-9098
          and tollfree 800 - 765-7379
EMAIL: info@childwellbeing.org
WEB: www.taskforce.org

The Collaborative Center for Child Well-Being,
established in 1999 as a program of the Task Force
on Child Survival and Development (founded in
1984), seeks to help develop local community infra-
structure to sustain an assets-based approach to
child well-being. The Center seeks to establish relationships with national organizations to facilitate
the integration of its work and its partners toward
sustained application of evidence-based strategies
through families, practitioners, childcare, schools
and communities. The Partnership Team works with
other organizations to identify and develop
resources and linkages to help communities build
effective systems to support positive child development in everyday life.

COMMISSION ON VOLUNTARY SERVICE & ACTION (CVSA)

P.O. Box 117
New York NY 10009
TEL/FAX: 718 - 638-8487

A consultative and coordinating body of non-governmental voluntary service organizations established
in 1945, CVSA publishes INVEST YOURSELF, a
comprehensive guide to full-time and part-time volunteer opportunities throughout North American

and the world, and a quarterly newsletter, *Items*,
for people involved in independent voluntary service
and action. INVEST YOURSELF is designed to reach
those willing to invest their most important resource
they own, themselves, in an effort to reverse the
devastating conditions facing people in the world
today, starting with fundamentals such as food,
health care, shelter, education, care for the aged
and disabled, environmental concerns and jobs at
a living wage. Also contact: CCIVS, Coordinating
Committee for International Voluntary Service,
1 Rue Miollis, 750 1055 France.

DR. REDDY'S FOUNDATION
Durganagar Colony, Panjagutta
Hyderabad 500 082 India
TEL: (91) 339-4603, -4613
FAX: (91) 339-4607

Founded in 1996 with the primary aim of helping
society reduce poverty, the Foundation fosters,
develops and promotes initiatives at individual,
group and organization levels that support sustainable environmental and economic development. It
has established three "social patents" using the
Foundation as a social catalyst; the Change Makers
Club, a forum for pooling ideas to better design
social experiments; and Mentoring, a modern version of the ancient Gurukula tradition where there is
one-to-one attention between teacher and pupil. The
Foundation's core programs include Child and Police
(CAP) Project, Street Kids Business School Program
(SKBS), Small Grants Program and Micro Finance
Entrepreneurs (MFE) Fellowship Support Program.

EARTHSAVE INTERNATIONAL
1509 Seabright Avenue, Suite B1

Santa Cruz CA 95062
TEL: 831 - 423-0293 or
         800 - 362-3648 (tollfree)
FAX: 831 - 423-1313
EMAIL: information@earthsave.org
WEB: www.earthsave.org

EarthSave, founded in 1988, is a nonprofit organization funded by membership fees, foundation grants, individual and corporate donations and program sponsorships. With chapters throughout the US and Canada, EarthSave promotes food choices that are healthy for people and for the planet. Its mission is to educate, inspire and empower people to shift toward a plant-based diet and to take compassionate action for all life on earth. Among its programs are potluck suppers, guided shopping tours, cooking classes, and support for parents on providing healthier food choices for their children at home and on advocating for the same at their children's schools. EarthSave publications include pamphlets on making the transition to vegetarian and vegan diets and a national quarterly newsletter. The program also provides videos, including "Diet for a New America," and speakers. EarthSave chapters organize participation in events such as Earth Day, Turkey-Free Thanksgiving and Taste of Health.

FAAF / FONDACION ARGENTINA DE APOYO FAMILIAR
Calle 33 No. 1978 La Plata
PCIA Buenos Aires Argentina
TEL/FAX: (54) 21 - 223-734
EMAIL: faafciaf@netverk.com.ar
WEB: www.netverk.com.ar/instituciones/
         apoyo_familiar

Founded in 1984, FAAF serves children age 3 to 13
from poor working families in Argentina. The organization is private, ecumenical and apolitical and runs
107 self-governing centers in Argentina. These
include Children's Houses and Workshops for
teenagers that assist over 5,000 young people
nationwide. The centers provide extended-day childcare, nutritious food and activities that promote
healthy physical, mental and moral development.
Other programs at FAAF centers include adult literacy, preventive medicine and job search assistance,
as well as presentations on prevention of AIDS,
alcohol abuse and family violence. FAAF supports a
variety of micro-enterprises and trains unemployed
teenagers in housing construction. In September
1995, 23 representatives from ten Latin-American
countries - Bolivia, Peru, Brazil, Colombia,
Paraguay, Uruguay, Chile, Venezuela, Ecuador and
Mexico - met to form the Confederacion
Internacional de Apoyo Familiar (CIAF). CIAF will,
with assistance from FAAF, advise groups in each of
these countries as they develop autonomous national foundations using FAAF as a model.

FAMILIES AND WORK INSTITUTE

330 7th Avenue, 14th Floor
New York NY 10001
TEL: 212 - 465-2044
FAX: 212 - 465-8637
WEB: www.familiesandwork.org

Families and Work Institute is a non-profit organization, founded in 1989 and funded by major US
foundations and corporations, that addresses the
changing nature of work and family life. The
Institute is committed to finding research-based

strategies that foster mutually supportive connections among workplaces, families and communities. With staff representing a wide range of research backgrounds in areas encompassing work-life, brain development of young children, families and community, fatherhood, parenting, and early education and care, the Institute identifies emerging work-life issues, benchmarks solutions to work-life problems, and evaluates the impact of solutions on employees, their families, their communities and on the productivity of employers. Major activities include policy and worksite research, evaluation, technical assistance and publication of as many as a dozen research reports and other documents each year. The Families and Work Institute also organizes an annual work-family conference in conjunction with The Conference Board.

FAMILIES FIRST
99 Bishop Allen Drive
Cambridge MA 02139
TEL: 617 - 868-7687
FAX: 617 - 354-2902
EMAIL: famfirst@tiac.net
WEB: www.families-first.org

Families First was founded in 1988 by Wheelock College and the Boston Children's Museum to provide education and support to parents of all backgrounds and life circumstances so that they may raise children who will develop into healthy, productive and caring members of their communities. The organization also provides education and training to professionals from diverse disciplines who support today's families. Recognizing that no one program can do it all, Families First collaborates with other organizations in serving families and strengthening communities.

FAMILIS OMF / WOF
World Organization for Families
4837 rue Boyer, Suite 110
Montreal PQ Canada H2J 3E6
TEL: 514 - 527-8435 or
          877 - 527-8435 (toll-free)
FAX: 514 - 527-8816
EMAIL: familis@familis.org
WEB: www.familis.org

Founded in 1995, FAMILIS OMF / WOF World
Organization for Families is a membership organization that seeks to serve as "a place and a link at the
service of the families of the world." Its objectives
are: to bring together on a worldwide basis contributors working for the betterment of families; to
carry out research concerning families; to inform
members about all pertinent matters; to find, ana-
lyze, and circulate information on families, family
policies and management of family policies; and to
represent families and their interests. It holds a
General Assembly every two years (most recently
September 19-22, 2000 in Madrid). FAMILIS welcomes as members governments and state agencies,
universities and other educational institutions,
businesses, labor unions and family organizations,
as well as individuals and families.

FAMILYEDUCATION NETWORK
20 Park Plaza, Suite 1420
Boston MA 02116
TEL: 617 - 542-6500
FAX: 617 - 542-6564
WEB: www.familyeducation.com,
          teachervision.com,
          myschoolonline.com,
          infoplease.com

FamilyEducation Network develops and provides educational and child-development resources and services for millions of families, corporate employers, schools and communities. The company's network of websites represent the largest K-12 community of parents, educators and students on the Internet. Founded in 1990, FamilyEducation Network helps parents, schools and community organizations use online tools and other media to become more effectively involved in their children's education and overall development. FamilyEducation Network's consortium of public sector and private sector relationships fosters a unique and proprietary private/public partnership model specifically designed to assist the country's parents, schools and teachers.

FAMILYHOSTEL and INTERHOSTEL

University of New Hampshire Continuing Education
6 Garrison Avenue
Durham NH 03824
TEL: 800 - 733-9753 (toll-free)
          or 603 - 862-1147
FAX: 603 - 862-1113
EMAIL: learn.dce@unh.edu
WEB: www.learn.unh.edu

INTERHOSTEL, founded in 1980, and FAMILYHOSTEL, founded in 1991, are moderately priced group travel programs with scheduled activities that independent vacationers would have difficulty duplicating. They have the added benefit of being learning vacations. FAMILYHOSTEL programs are designed for families with school-aged children, especially ages eight to 15. Programs are one week to ten days in the US and other countries. Adults, either parents, grandparents or another relative, must come

145

with children. INTERHOSTEL, for adults age 50 and older, offers over 75 one- to two-week-long programs in the US and all over the world.

FAMILY SUPPORT AMERICA
20 N. Wacker Drive, Suite 1100
Chicago IL 60606
TEL: 312 - 338-0900
FAX: 312 - 338-1522
EMAIL: info@familysupportamerica.org
WEB: www.familysupportamerica.org

Family Support America, formerly Family Resource Coalition of America, grew out of a Family Resource Forum in 1981 and is now a national consulting and advocacy organization serving the movement to strengthen and empower families and communities in order to foster the optimal development of children, youth and families. The organization's members include community-based program providers, school personnel, human service professionals, scholars and policymakers, many of whom have formed state and local networks across the U.S. Family Support America publishes resources for the family support field, including a quarterly magazine, *America's Family Support Magazine* and host national family support conferences.

FAMILY RESTAURANT READING PROGRAM
37 Ellen Road
Stoneham MA 02180
TEL: 781 - 279-4787
FAX: 781 - 279-9073
EMAIL: BLichtman@aol.com
WEB: www.readingout.com

The Family Restaurant Reading Program provides restaurants with storybooks for children ages three to ten years to use while dining. Participating restaurants lend these books to their patrons, as an alternative to diversions such as crayons and place-mats or toys and trinkets. Our mission is to intro-duce book titles which are entertaining and educa-tional, and to create a positive reading experience for children and their caregivers.

FAMILY VAN
Renaissance Park
1135 Tremont Street, 5th Floor
Boston MA 02120-2178
TEL: 617 - 754-8750
FAX: 617 - 754-8755

Founded in 1992, the Family Van is dedicated to promoting and preserving the health of minority communities within Greater Boston and serves the uninsured, individuals with limited social supports, young families, the homeless, new immigrants and the poor. The Family Van services include basic medical screenings, counseling, health education (including family planning, parenting and general support), risk reduction aids, emergency supplies, and medical and social service referrals.

FOLDA-USA / Friends of Literacy for Deaf Action
2930 Craiglawn Road
Silver Spring MD 20904-1816
TTY: 301 - 572-5168
FAX: 301 - 572-4134
EMAIL: alhagameyer@juno.com

Founded in 1994, FOLDA-USA is a section of the National Association of the Deaf (NAD, founded in 1880). FOLDA-USA has over one hundred NAD members who support publications and activities developed by the Friends groups for the benefit of the Deaf community. At the biennial conference of the NAD (most recently in Norfolk, Virginia, July 2000) FOLDA-USA recognizes NAD members who are authors, poets, and community leaders. Contact FOLDA-USA for ideas and suggestions for observing annual Deaf events throughout the year and for a list of resources on literacy for the Deaf.

THE FOUNDATION FOR GRANDPARENTING
108 Farnham Road
Ojai CA 93023
(No TEL or FAX)
EMAIL: gpfound@trail.com
WEB: www.grandparenting.org

The Foundation For Grandparenting is a not-for-profit, tax-exempt corporation, founded in 1980 and dedicated to raising grandparent consciousness and grandparent identity. Through education, research, programs, communication and networking, the organization promotes the benefit of grandparenting and the involvement of grandparents as agents of positive change for families and society.

FOURTH WORLD MOVEMENT
7600 Willow Hill Drive
Landover MD 20785 US
TEL: 301 - 336-9489
EMAIL: fourthworld@erols.com
WEB: www.atd-fourthworld.org
            -and- www.tapori.org
-also-
BP 7726
F-95036 Cergy Pontoise Cedex France

ATD-Fourth World is an international association of volunteers who work with and on behalf of those who live in extreme poverty (ATD stands for "aide a toute détresse," meaning help for all distress.) Fourth World organizes various practical projects including international workcamps during summer and year-round street libraries and Fourth World People's University that enable people in poverty to learn and teach and others to learn about the volunteers' work and about the lives of those in extreme poverty. The Fourth World Movement publishes a journal and books about the lives of the very poor and about successful action to emerge from poverty. It also has an on-going project called Tapori involving story-telling, writing, art, science and computer workshops for children ages 5 to 14.

GLOBAL NOMADS INTERNATIONAL
P.O. Box 9584
Washington DC 20016
TEL: 202 - 466-2244
FAX: 202 - 499-7320
EMAIL: gni@igc.org
WEB: globalnomads.association.com

Global Nomads International (GNI) is a non-profit organization that exists to promote opportunities for global nomads of all ages and nationalities to explore the lifelong impact of their internationally-mobile childhood, and to affirm and act on their unique international experience for their own enrichment and that of the larger world community. GNI publishes a magazine, GNI Perspectives, conducts presentations, workshops and seminars, organizes an annual conference and encourages the formation of local global nomad groups.

GRANDPARENT INFORMATION CENTER of the AARP

601 E Street NW
Washington DC 20049
TEL: 202 - 434-2296 (English)
          and 202 - 434-2281 (Spanish)
FAX: 202 - 434-6466
EMAIL: member@aarp.org
          (you do not need to be a member)
WEB: www.aarp.org/getans/consumer/
          grandparents.html

The Grandparent Information Center of the American Association of Retired Persons (AARP) provides information and resources to help grandparents raising their children cope with their primary caregiver roles. The Center works with agencies across the United States in the child care, aging, legal services and family service fields. It serves as a clearinghouse where grandparents, parents and service providers can obtain information and referral to national and local resources.

GRANDPARENTING, see FOUNDATION FOR GRANDPARENTING

HARVARD FAMILY RESEARCH PROJECT

38 Concord Avenue
Cambridge MA 02138
TEL: 617 - 496-4304
FAX: 617 - 495-8594
EMAIL: hfrp_gse@harvard.edu
WEB: gseweb.harvard.edu/~hfrp

Founded in 1983, The Harvard Family Research Project (HFRP) conducts research on and evaluation of programs and policies that affect families with young children. The project works to increase the effectiveness of public and private organizations and of communities as they promote child development, student achievement, healthy family functioning, and community building. Its role is to build capacity and to support high performance through solid research and evaluation. The audiences for HFRP's work include policymakers, practitioners, philanthropists, and concerned individuals. Among its goals is to provide research-based information to guide the strategic direction of new and existing initiatives. Its publications include a quarterly newsletter, *The Evaluation Exchange.*

HOSTELLING INTERNATIONAL®
AMERICAN YOUTH HOSTELS
733 15th Street NW, Suite 840
TEL: 202 - 783-6161
FAX: 202 - 783-6171
EMAIL: hiayhserv@hiayh.org
WEB: www.hiayh.org

This organization and Hostelling International - Canada are nonprofit membership organizations founded in 1934 as national members of the International Youth Hostel Federation. The Federation consists of 60 national member associations and 13 associate organizations. Its mission is to promote the education of all young people of all nations, but especially young people of limited means, by encouraging in them a greater knowledge, love and care of the countryside and an appreciation of the cultural values of towns and cities in all parts of the world. To this end, Federation associations provide hostels or other accommodations open to all in order to promote better understanding among people within their own countries and abroad. HOSTELLING INTERNATIONAL® maintains a worldwide network of hearly 5,000 hostels in more than 70 countries.

iComm
P.O. Box 371
253 College Street
Toronto Ontario
Canada M5T 1R5
TEL: 416 - 410-4067
FAX: 416 - 429-4154
EMAIL: icomm@icomm.ca
WEB: www.iComm.ca

iComm is a non-profit, Internet-based organization that exists to help other non-profit, charitable and community organizations by giving them Internet services and volunteer support.

IMPROBABLE PLAYERS
P.O. Box 746
Watertown MA 02471-0746
TEL: 617 - 926-8124
FAX: 617 - 926-8315
EMAIL: players@players.org
WEB: www.players.org/players

The Improbable Players, founded in 1984, educate the public about the effects of alcohol and other drug abuse through original theater performances. The shows are effective and powerful because the actors are recovering alcoholics and addicts. The scenes are created from their real-life stories and dramatize the effects of substance abuse on the family and its relation to other problems such as HIV/AIDS and violence. The company has played to school groups from elementary grades through college as well as community organizations, businesses and conferences throughout the country.

INDEPENDENT SECTOR

1200 Eighteenth Street, Suite 200
Washington DC 20036
TEL: 202 - 467-6100
FAX: 202 - 467-6101
EMAIL: info@indepsec.org
WEB: www.independentsector.org

INDEPENDENT SECTOR is a national leadership forum, working to encourage philanthropy, volunteering, not-for-profit initiative and citizen action to better serve people and communities.

INTERNATIONAL ASSOCIATION FOR VOLUNTEER EFFORT / IAVE

400 Eye St. NW #800
Washington DC 20005
TEL: 202 - 729-8250
FAX: 202 - 729-8102
EMAIL: IAVE@iave.org
WEB: www.iave.org

IAVE was created in 1970 by a small group of volunteers from throughout the world who shared a deep belief in the importance of volunteering and the value of international exchange as a way to build bridges among people. IAVE is an international membership organization dedicated to promoting, strengthening and celebrating volunteering worldwide. It is a network organization, with individual and organizational members in over 95 countries. It is governed by an elected international board of directors. IAVE conducts World Volunteer Conferences every two years and, in alternate years, regional conferences throughout the world. In 2001, the International Year of Volunteers, it held its World Conference in Amsterdam with over 1500 participants.

INTERNATIONAL FEDERATION FOR PARENT EDUCATION (IFPE)

2120 Est Rue Sherbrooke 212
Montreal H2K 1C3 Quebec CANADA
TEL: 514 - 523-5677
FAX: 514 - 523-9999
EMAIL: fiep@sympatico.ca
-also-
1 Avenue Leon Journault
F-92318 Sevres Cedex France
TEL: (33) 14 - 507-2164
FAX: (33) 14 - 626-6927

The International Federation of Schools for Parents was founded in France in 1964. The development of this federation and its expansion led, in 1978, to its becoming the International Federation for Parent Education (IFPE). The IFPE currently brings together associations and organizations from more than 40 countries on five continents and presents international conferences for policy makers and practitioners on topics related to parenting in today's world. With a strong membership base in Europe and a growing presence in Latin America, especially Mexico, the IFPE seeks to stimulate participation in the United States and Canada. The organization has, for many years, had consultative status with the United Nations and regularly participates in deliberations of the UN Economic and Social Development Commission, UNESCO and UNICEF.

IRAN PARENT TEACHER ASSOCIATION
P.O. Box 13185-1637
Tehran Iran
TEL: (98) - 21 - 649-3342
FAX: (98) - 21 - 649-0735

The Parent Teacher Association of Iran is a government-sponsored organization that, in April 2000, hosted an international congress of the International Federation for Parent Education on "Civilization, Education and Family" with participants from eleven countries outside Iran.

ISLAMIC HUMANITARIAN SERVICE
153 Frederick St., Suite 101
Kitchener Ontario
N2H 2M2 Canada
TEL: 519 - 576-7111
FAX: 519 - 576-0129
EMAIL: ihs@easynet.ca
WEB: www.al-haqq.com

The Islamic Humanitarian Service was founded in 1990 and has several sections including the United Muslim Women of Canada, which runs food banks in Montreal, Toronto and Edmonton, as well as a prison visitors section and a welfare section that helps needy families. They have other charitable projects including water wells in India and Africa.

JOIN TOGETHER
441 Stuart Street
Boston MA 02116
TEL: 617 - 437-1500
FAX: 617 - 437-9394
EMAIL: info@jointogether.org
WEB: www.jointogether.org

Join Together, a project of the Boston University
School of Public Health, is a national resource for
communities working to reduce substance abuse
and gun violence.

JUNIOR ACHIEVEMENT
One Education Way
Colorado Springs CO 80906
TEL: 719 - 540-8000
FAX: 719 - 540-9150
WEB: www.ja.org -and- www.jaintl.org

Junior Achievement, founded in 1919, is a non-
profit economic education organization dedicated to
teaching children and young people, in kindergarten
through high school, a fundamental understanding
of the free enterprise system. Its programs, taught
by classroom volunteers from the business community, reach over three million students each year in
the U.S. and over one million students in over 103
other countries. Age-appropriate curricula is
designed to teach elementary students about their
roles as individuals, workers and consumers and to
prepare middle grade and high school students for
key economic and workforce issues they will face. In
addition, Junior Achievement programs teach
youngsters the importance of staying in school and
offers programs for youngsters who may have difficulty graduating from high school. Junior

Achievement's more than 76,000 classroom volunteers come from all walks of life and include business people, college students and retirees.

KIWANIS International
3636 Woodview Trace
Indianapolis IN 46268-3196
TEL: 317 - 875-8755
FAX: 317 - 879-0204
EMAIL: kiwanismail@kiwanis.org
WEB: www.kiwanis.org

Founded in 1915, Kiwanis International is an organization of local service clubs. Clubs focus their service on children and sponsorship of youth service clubs: Key Club, Circle K, Builders Club and K-Kids. Kiwanis has approximately 300,000 members in more than 8,000 clubs in 82 countries, giving $138 million (US) and 6 million volunteer hours for community service each year.

LA LECHE LEAGUE
1400 N. Meacham Road
P.O. Box 4079
Schaumburg IL 60168-4079
TEL: 847 - 519-7730
FAX: 847 - 519-0035
EMAIL: LLLHQ@llli.org
WEB: www.lalecheleague.org

This international, nonprofit, nonsectarian organization is dedicated to providing education, information, support and encouragement to women who want to breastfeed. All breastfeeding mothers, as well as future breastfeeding mothers, are welcome to come to our meetings or call our Leaders for breastfeeding help. We also provide health care pro-

fessionals with continuing education opportunities
and the latest research on lactation management.

LIONS CLUBS International
300 22nd Street
Oak Brook IL 60523-8842
TEL: 630 - 571-5466
FAX: 630 - 571-8890
EMAIL: lions@lionsclubs.org
WEB: www. lionsclubs.org

Lions are members of community service clubs, dedicated to the idea that the men and women who live
in a community are in the best position to know who
needs help and why. More than 44,000 strong, these
local clubs are part of the world's largest such
organization, with 1.4 million members serving in
more than 180 countries and areas. The association
is both non-political and non-sectarian. Founded in
1917, Lions are now best known for their sight-relat-
ed programs, including SightFirst, the world's largest
blindness prevention program. Lions Clubs
International Foundation (LCIF) is the charitable
arm of Lions Clubs International (LCI). The foundation's mission is to support the efforts of Lions clubs
around the world in serving their local and global
communities by funding humanitarian service projects. In 1998 LCIF approved more than US$13.9 mil-
lion in grants for Lions' districts around the world.

LIVESAFE FOUNDATION
P.O. Box 157
Boston MA 02134
TEL: 617 - 734-6375
FAX: 617 - 232-1844
EMAIL: livesafe@ livesafe.org
WEB: www.livesafe.org

Founded in 1995, the LiveSafe Foundation is a non-profit organization serving economically disadvantaged children, teens and adults (both male and female, ages 4 to 84) in Greater Boston and other New England communities with programs to break the cycle of violence and abuse in society. It offers personal safety training, using the Impact Model Mugging curriculum, in collaboration with schools, after-school programs, community centers and shelters. The programs teach people to keep themselves safe from violence in their homes and communities.

MEXICAN NATIONAL PARENTS ASSOCIATION
See ANPAF

MOTHERS & MORE
P.O. Box 31
Elmhurst, IL 60126
TEL: 630 - 941-3553
FAX: 630 - 941-3551
WEB: www.mothersandmore.org

Mothers & More, founded in 1987 as FEMALE ("formerly employed mothers at the leading edge"), is an international non-profit membership organization for women who have altered their career paths in order to care for their children at home, referred to as "sequencing mothers." Mothers & More addresses women's personal needs and interests during their active parenting years. Mothers & More promotes recognition and respect for "sequencing mothers" and respects the right of every mother to choose if and how she will combine parenting and paid employment. Mothers & More advocates for public policies and employment policies that accommodate "sequencing," the term used to describe a mother's withdrawing from or reducing her time in the paid workforce in order to care for her children. Thirty-four percent of Mothers & More members currently work for pay in some capacity. The organization has over 175 chapters and 7000-plus members world-wide (in all but three of the fifty United States, in Australia, Belgium, Brazil, Canada, Denmark, Germany, Japan, Poland, Puerto Rico, Switzerland and the U.K.). Mothers & More publishes a bi-monthly newsletter on concerns related to support, advocacy, work trends and women's unity.

NATIONAL ASSOCIATION OF THE DEAF

814 Thayer Avenue
Silver Spring MD 20910-4500
TTY: 301 - 587-1789
TEL: 301 - 587-1788
FAX: 301 - 587-1791
EMAIL: nadinfo@nad.org
WEB: www.nad.org

Founded in 1880, the National Association of the Deaf (NAD) is the oldest and largest organization representing people with disabilities in the United States. The NAD safeguards the accessibility and civil rights of 28 million Deaf and hard of hearing Americans in a variety of areas including education, employment, health care and social services, and telecommunications. A private, non-profit organization, the NAD is a federation of 51 state association affiliates, sponsoring and organizational affiliates, and direct members. Program and activities include grassroots advocacy and empowerment, captioned media, certification of American Sign Language professionals, certification of sign language interpreters, deafness-related information and publications, legal assistance, policy development and research, public awareness, and youth leadership development.

NATIONAL CENTER FOR FATHERING
10200 W. 75th Street, Suite 267
Shawnee Mission KS 66210-2223
TEL: 913 - 384-4661
          800 - 593-3237
FAX: 913 - 384-4665
EMAIL: dads@fathers.com
WEB: www.fathers.com

Founded in 1990 as a response to the growing trend toward fatherlessness, the National Center for Fathering seeks to champion the role of responsible fatherhood by inspiring and equipping men to be more engaged in the lives of their children. It relies on cutting-edge research to produce practical resources for fathers. These resources serve as the basis for the Center's core competency: father training. The Center offers a range of courses for fathers including two-day community-wide seminars for up to 1,500, multi-week curricula for small groups of dads and Train the Trainer programs to equip leaders to use the Center's curriculum in their own presentations. The National Center for Fathering also produces a daily, three-minute radio program and publishes a quarterly "how-to"-oriented magazine called *Today's Father*.

NATIONAL CHILDREN'S BUREAU
8 Wakley Street
London EC1V 7QE United Kingdom
TEL: (44) 207 - 843-6099
FAX: (44) 207 - 843-6323
EMAIL: library@ncb.org.uk

A long-established national (UK) organization that publishes materials on child development and presents conferences for professionals who work with children.

NATIONAL FAMILY CAREGIVERS ASSOCIATION

10605 Concord Street, Suite 501
Kensington MD 20895-2504
TEL: 800 - 896-3650 / 301 - 942-5430
FAX: 301 - 942-2302
EMAIL: info@nfcacares.org
WEB: www.nfcacares.org

NFCA, founded in 1993, is dedicated to making life better for all of America's family caregivers: more than 25 million people who find themselves in a caregiving role. Family caregivers focus on their loved one's needs. NFCA focuses on family caregivers. NFCA espouses a philosophy of empowerment and self-care that is predicated on the belief that caregivers who choose to take charge of their lives, and see caregiving as but one of its facets, are in a position to be happier and healthier individuals. NFCA's member programs include a caregiver-to-caregiver peer support network, National Family Caregivers Month, celebrated each year during November, resource referrals, special reports and educational materials, and a bereavement program for former caregivers. Membership includes a quarterly newsletter, Take Care!

NATIONAL FATHERHOOD INITIATIVE

101 Lake Forest Blvd., Suite 360
Gaithersburg MD 20878
TEL: 301 - 948-0599
FAX: 301 - 948-4325
EMAIL: nfi1995@aol.com
WEB: www.fatherhood.org

The National Fatherhood Initiative (NFI) was created in 1994 to improve the well-being of children by increasing the number of children growing up with loving, committed and responsible fathers. A non-profit, non-sectarian, non-partisan organization, NFI conducts public awareness campaigns promoting responsible fatherhood, organizes conferences and community fatherhood forums, provides resource material to organizations seeking to establish support programs for fathers, publishes a quarterly newsletter, and disseminates informational material to men seeking to become more effective fathers.

NATIONAL INSTITUTE ON MEDIA AND THE FAMILY
606 24th Avenue South, Suite 606
Minneapolis MN 55454
TEL: 612 - 672-5437 or
          toll-free 888 - 672-5437 (672-KIDS)
FAX: 612 - 672-4113
EMAIL: webmaster@mediafamily.org
WEBSITE: www.mediaandthefamily.org

Founded in 1996, the Institute is a nonprofit, national resource center for research, information and education about the impact of the media on children and families. It seeks to maximize the benefits and minimize the harm of media on children and families and provides educational tools and materials to help parents, teachers, community leaders and other caring adults understand the impact of the media, so they can make informed choices for children. The Institute is not affiliated with any political or religious organization and does not endorse censorship of any kind. The Institute puts considerable emphasis on violence in the media because studies have shown, and experts agree, that a reduction of violence in the media will not only reduce violence on our streets, it will reduce the cost of healthcare by as much as 25 percent. The Institute is funded through grants from foundations and corporations and donations from individuals.

NATIONAL PARENTING ASSOCIATION
51 West 74th Street, Suite 1-B
New York NY 10023-2495
TEL: 212 - 362-7575
FAX: 212 - 362-1916
EMAIL: info@parentsunite.org
WEB: www.parentsunite.org

The National Parenting Association, founded in 1993 to give parents a greater public voice, listens to parents through surveys, website and its state partner network; advocates for public and private initiatives giving parents practical support; informs parents about issues and helps them make their voices heard; promotes positive images of parents and parenting through publications, website and media campaigns; and engages community, business and union leaders with scholars in round table discussions on the role that private and public sectors can play in supporting parents.

NATIONAL PARENTING EDUCATION NETWORK (NPEN)
(see also PEN of Massachusetts)
c/o ERIC Clearinghouse
UIUC Children's Research Center
51 Gerty Drive
Champaign IL 61820-7469
TEL: 800 - 583-4135
FAX: 217 - 333-3767
EMAIL: npen@ericps.crc.uiuc.edu
WEB: http://npen.crc.uiuc.edu

The National Parenting Education Network (NPEN) is a national (US) professional organization whose mission is to advance the field of parenting education. Many professionals from a variety of fields including education, health care, social work, and religious and volunteer organizations are involved with the practice of parenting education and the organization promotes a multidisciplinary approach to parenting education. The organization began informally in 1995 and became known as the Parenting Education Network (PEN). After meetings with representatives of various existing organizations such as National Conference on Family Relations (NCFR), Family Resource Coalition (FRC), and National Parent Instructors Association (NPIA) to discuss and explore possible relationships, NPEN was formally organized in 1997.

NATIONAL PARENTING INFORMATION NETWORK (NPIN)
UIUC Children's Research Center
51 Gerty Drive
Champaign IL 61820-7469
TEL: 800 - 583-4135
FAX: 217 - 333-3767
EMAIL: askeece@uiuc.edu
WEB: www.npin.org

The National Parent Information Network (NPIN) is a project sponsored by two Educational Resources Information Centers (ERIC) clearinghouses: the ERIC Clearinghouse on Urban Education (Teachers College, Columbia University, New York City) and the ERIC Clearinghouse on Elementary and Early Childhood Education (University of Illinois at Urbana-Champaign). All other ERIC system components are also contributors and participants. Many

165

collaborating organizations provide information resources to NPIN and promote use of NPIN among their constituencies. The purpose of NPIN is to provide information to parents and those who work with parents and to foster the exchange of parenting materials. Materials included in full text on NPIN have been reviewed for reliability and usefulness.

NATIONAL PTA (PARENT TEACHER ASSOCIATION)

330 N. Wabash Avenue, Suite 2100
Chicago IL 60611
TEL: 800 - 307-4782 toll-free
        -or- 312 - 670-6782
FAX: 312 - 670-6783
EMAIL: info@pta.org
WEB: www.pta.org

The National PTA, founded in 1897, is a volunteer association with 6.5 million members, working exclusively on behalf of children and youth. Through local affiliates, the PTA seeks to fulfill its three-fold mission: to support and speak on behalf of children and youth in the schools, in the community and before governmental bodies and other organizations that make decisions affecting children; to assist parents in developing the skills they need to raise and protect their children; and to encourage parent and public involvement in the public schools of this nation.

NATIONAL TENPOINT LEADERSHIP FOUNDATION

Ella J. Baker House
411 Washington Street
Boston MA 02124
TEL: 617 - 282-6704

FAX: 617 - 822-1832
WEBSITE: www.ntlf.org

Founded in 1997, the National TenPoint Leadership Foundation's (NTLF) mission is to assist local faith-based organizations to intervene in violent aspects of youth culture to reduce crime, especially in the major urban centers of the United States. In addition to the Ella J. Baker House in Boston, Massachusetts, affiliates currently include those in Providence, Rhode Island; Gary and Indianapolis, Indiana; Tulsa, Oklahoma; and Brooklyn, New York. Other organizations are using TenPoint principles in their programming although they are not directly affiliated with NTLF. The organization's Operation 2006 provides support for high-risk youth through close collaboration with local law enforcement agencies and recognized social service agencies. The pilot of this program is being run by the Ella J. Baker House of Boston in Dorchester, Massachusetts.

NGO Committee on the Family - Vienna
Martinstrasse 92/3 first floor
A-1180 Vienna
TEL: (43) 1 - 405-8901
EMAIL: peter.crowley@t-online.de or
          ematt@vki.or.at

Sponsored by the United Nations, governments, regional associations, and other donors since the U.N. International Year of the Family 1994, this Committee publishes an information-sharing quarterly bulletin, *Families International*. The Vienna Committee promotes and publicizes

celebrations of International Day of Families on
May 15th and other family-related activities.

OTEF - ORGANIZATION TUNISIENNE DE L'E-
DUCATION ET DE LA FAMILLE / Tunisia
78, Av. de la Liberté
1002 Tunis Tunisia
TEL: (216) 1 - 845-410 -or- 848-133
FAX: (216) 1 - 783-594

OTEF supports the education of children and young
people and encourages parents to take an active
role in their children's learning. The organization
has 27 regional bureaus in Tunisia and is active
nationally as a member of numerous Tunisian state
councils and offices. OTEF is a member of a number
of regional (North African, Arab and African) associations and of other international organizations
including the International Federation for Parent
Education. OTEF also has consultative status with
the United Nations Economic and Social
Development Commission.

PARENTAL STRESS LINE
Parents' and Children's Services
654 Beacon Street
Boston MA 02215
TEL: 617 - 528-5800
FAX: 617 - 528-5880
EMAIL: info@pcs.org
WEB: www.pcsonline.org

Founded in 1849, Parents' and Children's Services
of The Children's Mission (PCS) is an agency committed to the well-being of children, families and
communities. Services include telephone helplines,
family preservation programs, mental health services, education, and juvenile justice intervention. The

mission of Parents' and Children's Services is to promote the well-being of children and the preservation of families through culturally competent direct service, education, and advocacy.

PARENTING COALITION INTERNATIONAL
1025 Connecticut Avenue NW, Suite 415
Washington DC 20036
TEL: 202 - 530-0849
FAX: 202 - 989-1155 / 404 - 551-7881
EMAIL: brollins@parentingcoalition.org
WEBSITE: www.parentingcoalition.org

Parenting Coalition International (PCI), formerly known as the National Parents' Day Coalition, was founded in 1994 and is a membership organization for parenting professionals, parents, organizations, agencies, churches and faith-based groups. PCI presently has over 250 individual and organizational members in five countries and some of the organizations who belong to PCI themselves have memberships in the thousands. The organization works to ensure that all parents have access to the knowledge, tools and resources for raising healthy, successful and responsible children. It celebrates good parenting and the role of models who embody good parenting. PCI solicits nominations for a series of awards, given each year, in various categories related to parenting and parent education, and organizes annual satellite cablecast discussions on parenting resources and parenting education topics.

PARENTING EDUCATION NETWORK
see NATIONAL PARENTING
EDUCATION NETWORK

PARENTING EDUCATION NETWORK
of Massachusetts
P.O. Box 618
Belmont MA 02178
TEL: 617 - 253-9467
EMAIL: pen_m@yahoo.com

The mission of the Parenting Education Network of
Massachusetts (formerly known as Professionals for
Parents and Families / PPF) is to strengthen the
field of parenting education by promoting networking opportunities and professional development for
those who are involved in parenting education and
family support. PEN welcomes members into a circle
of colleagues and friends, offering speaker series,
conferences and training, networking events, study
groups and educational programs.

PARENTING EDUCATION & SUPPORT FORUM
Unit 431 Highgate Studios
53-79 Highgate Road
London NW5 1TL United Kingdom
TEL: (44) 207 - 284-8370
FAX: (44) 207 - 485-3587
EMAIL: pesf@dial.pipex.com
WEB: www.parenting-forum.org.uk

The Parenting Education & Support Forum (PESF)
grew out of the National Children's Bureau, becoming independent in 1999. PESF publishes *The
Parenting Forum Newsletter* and is the national
provider in the UK of information and support to
practitioners. Its role is to support, inform and represent those working with parents. It offers training
and networking opportunities and is the key source
of feedback to national policy-makers on the impact
of the new initiatives and the interaction between

providers at local levels. In partnership with PAULO (named after Paulo Friere, the celebrated South American community educator), a national training organization for community-based learning and development, PESF is developing national quality standards for working with parents.

The PARENTING JOURNEY
The Family Center
385 Highland Avenue
Somerville MA 02144.
TEL: 617 - 628-8815
FAX: 617 - 625-2351

The Parenting Journey, a parenting education program, was founded in 1997 using a therapeutic family systems model. To date over 250 facilitators representing more than 150 agencies have been trained in the model in New England and New York. A five-day training prepares clinicians to facilitate the 12-session program that concentrates on emotional understanding of what it means to be a parent. Certification programs and publications offered by The Family Center support the work of Parenting Journey facilitators in various locations.

PARENTS ANONYMOUS
675 W. Foothill Boulevard, Suite 220
Claremont CA 91711-3475
TEL: 909 - 621-6184
FAX: 909 - 625-6304
EMAIL: parentsanon@msn.com
WEB: www.parentsanonymous-natl.org

Parents Anonymous was founded in 1970 through the efforts of a mother seeking to help create a safe, caring home for her family. Working in partnership with her social worker, they launched a national movement to bring help, support, strength and hope to millions of families all across America. Their vision inspired thousands of parents, professional and community volunteers to establish Parents Anonymous groups throughout the US. PA is the nation's oldest and largest child abuse prevention organization dedicated to strengthening families through innovative strategies that promote mutual support and parent leadership.

PARENTS, FAMILIES AND FRIENDS OF LESBIANS AND GAYS (PFLAG)
1101 14th Street NW, Suite 1030
Washington DC 20005
TEL: 202 - 638-4200
FAX: 202 - 638-0243
EMAIL: info@pflag.org
WEB: www.pflag.org

PFLAG is a national nonprofit organization with a membership of over 77,000 households and more than 425 affiliates worldwide. This grassroots network is developed and served by the PFLAG national office, located in Washington, DC, a national Board of Directors and Regional Directors' Council. The organization promotes the health and well-being of gay, lesbian, bisexual and transgendered persons, their families and friends through support and advocacy. Parents, Families and Friends of Lesbians and Gays provides opportunity for dialogue about sexual orientation and gender identity, and acts to create a society that is healthy and respectful of human diversity.

PARENTS FORUM
144 Pemberton Street
Cambridge MA 02140-2509
TEL: 671 - 864-3802

EMAIL: info@parentsforum.org
WEB: www.parentsforum.org

A solution-oriented, assets-based program of networking, skill development and support for parents and others caring for children, founded in 1992, PARENTS FORUM is open to everyone concerned about healthier family life. We organize book and toy exchanges to benefit local agencies serving families, present workshops on parenting issues using our eight (agenda) questions and continue to develop creative, workable solutions to the challenges of contemporary parenting. We collaborate with other organizations, local, national and international, to raise awareness of parents' concerns.

PARENTS HELPING PARENTS
The Roundtable of Support
140 Clarendon Street
Boston MA 02116
TEL: 617 - 267-8077 and
               tollfree 800 - 882-1250
FAX: 617 - 266-9837

Parents Helping Parents: The Roundtable of Support is committed to strengthening families throughout Massachusetts. Parent members, volunteers and staff run sixty weekly support groups, a counseling and referral hotline, conferences and parent leadership training. Group meetings are parent-run, with trained volunteers, many of whom have a professional background in social services, facilitating the discussions. Parents share their difficulties and successes, help each other sort through their frustrations, and explore different ways of dealing with situations that seem overwhelming. Parents help each other as well as themselves and forge connections that can last a lifetime.

PARENTS TELEVISION COUNCIL
600 Wiltshire Boulevard, Suite 700
Los Angeles CA 90017
TEL: 213 - 629-9255
FAX: 213 - 629-9254
EMAIL: mrc@mediaresearch.org
WEB: www.parentstv.org

The Parents Television Council (PTC) was established in 1995 as the Hollywood project of the Media Research Center. The PTC offers private sector solutions to restore television to its roots as an independent and socially responsible entertainment medium. The PTC motivates the public to voice its support of family-friendly programming to network executives, advertisers, public policy leaders, and the creative community in Hollywood. The PTC has employed these efforts to help save values-driven shows such as CBS's Touched By An Angel and Dr. Quinn, Medicine Woman. Using scientific analysis generated from the Media Research Center's computerized Media Tracking System (MTS), the PTC publishes Special Reports focusing on a variety of topics relating to the content of prime time television, including in-depth analyses of the "family hour" and the new television ratings system, and an annual Family Guide to Prime Time Television.

PARENTS WITHOUT PARTNERS
1650 South Dixie Highway, Suite 510
Boca Raton, FL 33432
TEL: 561 - 391-8833
FAX: 561 - 395-8557

EMAIL: pwp@jti.net
WEB: www.parentswithoutpartners.org

This international nonprofit educational organization, founded in 1957, is devoted to the interests of single parents and their children. Through the exchange of ideas and companionship, it helps its members deal with the problems they face in bringing up children alone, contending with the emotional conflicts of divorce, never-married, separation or widowhood. PWP Inc. provides discussions, professional speakers, study groups, publications and social activities for families and adults. Of its 50,000+ members in the United States and Canada, ranging in age from 18 to 80, 55% are female and 45% male.

PHARE Pour l'Harmonie des Relations Enfant-Parents
13, rue Caumartin
F-75009 Paris France
TEL: (33) 142 - 66-5555
TEL: (33) 142 - 66-5099

PHARE is a French non-profit organization established in 1991 to foster harmonious relationships between parents and children. Its principal purpose is prevention of suicide among young people.

PRODDER Programme for Development Research
P O Box 32410
2017 Braamfontein
South Africa
TEL: (27) 11 - 482-6150
FAX: (27) 11 - 482-4739
EMAIL: DBB@zeus.hsrc.ac.za or

YOF@zeus.hsrc.ac.za
WEB: www.prodder.co.za/

PRODDER (Programme for Development Research) seeks to provide appropriate, comprehensive and dynamic development information to people and organizations. With the South African National NGO Coalition, which works for people-centered development, participatory democracy and a strong voluntary sector, PRODDER disseminates a weekly e-mail development information newsletter.

PROJECT PARENTS
24 Appleton Street
Boston MA 02116
TEL: 617 - 451-0360
WEB: www.projectparents.org

Project Parents, first organized in 1990, provides educational programs to increase the effectiveness and involvement of urban parents in the educational lives of their children. It consults with city government officials, public schools and housing authorities; trains teachers, bilingual representatives and concerned citizens in Project Parents workshops; conducts workshops for parents in public schools and at housing developments; consults with housing authorities about establishing after-school reading programs and on-site libraries in community and youth centers; and produces educational videos for parents, including Read, It's Fun! Project Parents workshops are on such topics as reading at home, parent-teacher partnership, listening to children, and parents helping parents.

PTA See NATIONAL PTA

RESPECT FOR PARENTS DAY

P.O. Box 1563
Lancaster CA 93539
TEL/FAX: 661 - 945-2360
EMAIL: marilyn@rglobal.net
WEB: http://members.tripod.com/
          MarilynDalrymple/index-4.html

This initiative, begun in 1993, establishes August 1st of each year as Respect for Parents Day and seeks endorsement of community members and leaders throughout the United States and around the world.

ROTARY International

One Rotary Center
1560 Sherman Avenue
Evanston IL 60201
TEL: 847 - 866-3000
FAX: 847 - 328-8554
WEB: www.rotary.org

Rotary is a worldwide organization of business and professional leaders who provide humanitarian service, encourage high ethical standards in all vocations and help build goodwill and peace in the world. There are approximately 1-2 million Rotarians, members of more than 29,000 Rotary Clubs in 160 countries. Under the auspices of Rotary International and The Rotary Foundation, Rotarians around the world participate in and administer a broad range of humanitarian and educational programs including scholarships, cultural exchanges, and opportunities for service at the local, national and international levels.

SAMARITANS / SAMARITEENS
Suicide Prevention
500 Commonwealth Avenue
Boston MA 02215
TEL: 617 - 247-0220 - 24-hour hotline
TEL: 617 - 247-8050 or
        800 - 252-8336 - teens only
TEL: 617 - 536-2460 - business office
FAX: 617 - 247-0207

Founded in April 1974, the Samaritans provides a free and confidential 24-hour telephone befriending line, staffed by trained volunteers, offering unconditional and non-judgmental support to those who are alone, depressed or in crisis, no matter what the challenge or struggle. The program also offers SafePlace, an open, confidential support group for individuals who have lost loved ones to suicide. Samaritans provide education and training on identifying those at risk for suicide, and on suicide prevention strategies, to schools, professional groups and other organizations. It also has two special programs: Samariteens, dedicated to assisting teens in despair, and Lifeline, a suicide prevention and intervention program in selected Eastern Massachusetts correctional facilities.

See also BEFRIENDERS and SPAN
SPAN - Suicide Prevention Awareness Network
5034 Odin's Way
Marietta GA 30068
TEL: 888 - 649-1366
FAX: 770 - 642-1419
EMAIL: act@spanusa.org
LISTSERVE: spanusa@lists.best.com
WEB: www.spanusa.org

SPAN, founded in 1996, links the energy of those bereaved by suicide, and those who have attempted suicide, with the expertise of leaders in public health, mental health, science, business, government and public service to achieve the goal of significantly reducing suicide on a sustainable basis by the year 2010. It works for the implementation of a National Suicide Prevention Strategy through active collaboration of all groups and people interested in suicide prevention and the reduction of suicidal behavior.

TOUGHLOVE® International

P.O. Box 1069
Doylestown PA 18901
TEL: 800 - 333-1069
FAX: 215 - 348-9874
EMAIL: service@toughlove.org
WEB: www.toughlove.org

TOUGHLOVE® International is a non-profit organization for parents troubled by their children's behavior. The program's goal is to stop destructive behavior in families and communities by developing the power of adults and young people. There are over 500 volunteer-led affiliated groups in North and South America, Europe and Asia, with parents of teenagers, preteens and adult children, as well as grandparents.

TUNISIAN ORGANIZATION FOR EDUCATION AND THE FAMILY
see OTEF

TV FREE AMERICA

1611 Connecticut Avenue NW, Suite 3A
Washington DC 20009
TEL: 202 - 887-0436

FAX: 202 - 518-5560
EMAIL: tvfa@essential.org
WEB: www.tvfa.org

TV-Free America is a national, nonprofit, nonpartisan organization that encourages Americans to reduce, voluntarily and dramatically, the amount of television they watch in order to promote richer, healthier and more connected lives, families and communities. It promotes an annual TV-Turnoff Week each April and publishes a quarterly newsletter for individual and corporate members.

UNITED NATIONS Family Unit
Room DC2-1302
Two United Nations Plaza
New York NY 10017
TEL: 212 - 963-3238
FAX: 212 - 963-3062
EMAIL: ghaleb@un.org
WEB: www.un.org

Under the Secretariat of the Division for Social Policy and Development, the UN Family Unit supports the worldwide observance of the International Day of Families, May 15th, by preparing background information on the family for use by governments, the United Nations and non-profit or non-governmental organizations (NGOs). The Secretariat also supports action-oriented research on family issues. During 1998-1999, in cooperation with the International Federation of Training and Development Organizations, the Family Unit conducted A Survey of National Family Policies in Argentina, Egypt,

India and the Netherlands that focused on the issue of balance between work and family responsibilities and the need for family-friendly policies in the workplace. Another publication, Selected Country Profiles on Family Policies and Programs, is in preparation describing national actions on family-related issues in Austria, Cameroon, Jamaica and the Republic of Korea. The Secretariat has strengthened the consultative process with NGOs at all levels. With financial assistance from the UN Trust Fund on Family Activities, the Family Unit allocates grants for activities specific to families with a special focus on least developed and developing countries and countries with economies in transition. The Secretariat encourages research with a focus on policy relevance and is establishing an inter-university network on family policy development. In 2004 the Family Unit will plan and coordinate a celebration of the tenth anniversary of the 1994 International Year of the Family.

VIVA RIO
Rua Barao, 207 - Praca Seca
Jacarepagua CEP 21321-620
Rio de Janeiro RJ Brazil
TEL: 55 - 21 - 3350-8342
FAX: 55 - 21 - 9701-9631
EMAIL: info@vivario.org.br
WEB: www.vivario.org.br

Viva Rio was founded in 1993 and works in more than 500 favelas and low-income communities in Rio de Janeiro's Metropolitan Area, focusing its violence prevention activities on youth. The organization develops and administers programs in five major areas: human rights and public safety, education, sports, community development and income generation and the environment. The criteria for its projects are that: one, they should have clear results; two, they should have the potential for wide-scale implementation and three, they should strengthen local associations. Presently there are 900 volunteers and 1100 paid employees in Viva Rio projects.

VOLUNTEER SOLUTIONS Inc.
c/o Virtual Ink
56 Roland Street, Suite 306
Boston MA 02129
TEL: 617 - 921-1849
FAX: 617 - 623-9965
EMAIL: info@volunteersolutions.org
WEB: www.volunteersolutions.org

Volunteer Solutions promotes volunteerism across all sectors of society with an online database of volunteer opportunities available at no cost to either volunteers or nonprofit agencies. The program also connects universities, corporations, and other membership organizations with each other through partnership programs and promotes their volunteer activities with a custom-designed interface to the Volunteer Solutions database. Also Volunteer Solutions connects registered users with one another through distinct online communities. Founded in 1998, Volunteer Solutions presently serves five cities across the United States. It is funded by grants and donations.

WORLD LEARNING
Kipling Road
P.O. Box 676
Brattleboro VT 05302-0676
TEL: 802 - 258-3143
FAX: 802 - 258-3248

EMAIL: info@worldlearning.org
WEB: www.worldlearning.org

Founded in 1932 as The Experiment in International Living, World Learning is a global organization promoting international understanding, education and partnerships. It offers summer abroad, college semester abroad, and group homestay programs, as well as multicultural learning and language training (at its School for International Training) and projects in international development and training.

YOUNG AUDIENCES Inc.

115 East 92nd Street
New York NY 10128-1688
TEL: 212 - 831-8110
FAX: 212 - 289-1202
WEB: www.ya.org

Since 1952, Young Audiences (YA) has been presenting performing and visual artists to young people through a network that now includes 33 chapters and affiliated organizations throughout the United States. Each year the program selects 4,000 professional artists, presents 83,000 programs and reaches 7 million young people. The Young Audience national organization certifies YA chapters for program quality, provides a wide range of services and advocates quality arts education for all children.

SEVERAL ADDITIONAL WEBSITES

www.acf.dhhs.gov
U.S. Government Administration for Children and Families

www.ala.org/parentspage
American Library Association Parents Page

www.helpfamilies.org
Cambridge Family and Children's Service

www.childrenspartnership.org
The Children's Partnership

www.civitas.org
Tools for Shaping Children's Lives

www.ed.gov/pubs/parents/internet
U.S. Department of Education, Parents' Guide to the Internet

www.familyinfoserve.com
Professional development for parenting and family life educators

www.hampton.va.us/healthyfamilies/
Hampton (VA) partnership for healthy families

www.hsph.harvard.edu/chc/parenting
Harvard School of Public Health Parenting Project two online reports: Raising Teens and The Role of Mass Media in Parenting Education

www.iamyourchild.org
National campaign to make early childhood development a top priority

www.jumpstart.org
Coalition for personal financial literacy

www.kidsindanger.org
Information on unsafe products for children

www.parentingpublications.org
National trade association of regional parenting
publications

www.parentsjournal.com
National radio series of interviews on parenting
issues

www.parentsjourney.com
Online information and support for parenting

www.parentleaders.org
Parents Leadership Institute addresses personal
challenges and
societal conditions that make parenting a struggle

www.zerotothree.org
National Center for Infants, Toddlers and Families

LIST — All in the US except as noted.

ALGEBRA PROJECT
ALLIANCE FOR CHILDHOOD
AMERICAN TOY INSTITUTE
ASSOCIAÇION NACIONAL DE PADRES DE FAMILIA
   México
ASPIRA ASSOCIATION
AT-HOME DAD
BECAUSE I LOVE YOU
BEFRIENDERS INTERNATIONAL United Kingdom
BUSINESS FOR SOCIAL RESPONSIBILITY
CAMBRIDGE FAMILY LITERACY COLLABORATIVE
CAMBRIDGE SENIOR VOLUNTEER
   CLEARINGHOUSE
CHAMBER OF COMMERCE of Cambridge
CHAMBER OF COMMERCE of Somerville
CHARACTER COUNTS! sm
CHILD GROUP THERAPY ASSOCIATION
CHILDREN'S DEFENSE FUND
CHILDREN'S TRUST FUND
CONFEDERACION INTERNACIONAL DE APOYO
   FAMILIAR
-- See FEDERACION ARGENTINA PARA APOYO
   FAMILIAR Argentina
CIVICUS
COLLABORATIVE CENTER FOR CHILD WELL-
   BEING
COMMISSION ON VOLUNTARY SERVICE & ACTION
DR. REDDY'S FOUNDATION India
EARTHSAVE
FONDACION ARGENTINA DE APOYO FAMILIAR
   Argentina
FAMILIES AND WORK INSTITUTE
FAMILIES FIRST
FAMILIS Canada
FAMILYEDUCATION NETWORK
FAMILYHOSTEL and INTERHOSTEL

FAMILY SUPPORT AMERICA
FAMILY RESTAURANT READING PROGRAM
FAMILY VAN
FOLDA / Friends of Literacy for Deaf Action
The FOUNDATION FOR GRANDPARENTING
FOURTH WORLD MOVEMENT
GLOBAL NOMADS INTERNATIONAL
GRANDPARENT INFORMATION CENTER of the
　AARP
GRANDPARENTING -- See FOUNDATION FOR
　GRANDPARENTING
HARVARD FAMILY RESEARCH PROJECT
HOSTELLING INTERNATIONAL® AMERICAN
　YOUTH HOSTELS
iComm
IMPROBABLE PLAYERS
INDEPENDENT SECTOR
INTERNATIONAL ASSOCIATION FOR VOLUNTEER
　EFFORT
INTERNATIONAL FEDERATION FOR PARENT
　EDUCATION France and Canada
IRAN PARENT TEACHER ASSOCIATION Iran
ISLAMIC HUMANITARIAN SERVICE Canada
JOIN TOGETHER
JUNIOR ACHIEVEMENT
KIWANIS International
LA LECHE LEAGUE
LIONS CLUBS International
LIVESAFE FOUNDATION
MEXICAN NATIONAL PARENTS ASSOCIATION --
　See ANPAF Mexico
MOTHERS & MORE
NATIONAL ASSOCIATION OF THE DEAF
NATIONAL CENTER FOR FATHERING
NATIONAL CHILDREN'S BUREAU United Kingdom
NATIONAL FAMILY CAREGIVERS ASSOCIATION
NATIONAL FATHERHOOD INITIATIVE
NATIONAL INSTITUTE ON MEDIA AND THE FAMILY

NATIONAL PARENTING ASSOCIATION
NATIONAL PARENTING EDUCATION NETWORK
   See also PEN of Massachusetts
NATIONAL PARENTING INFORMATION NETWORK
NATIONAL PARENT TEACHER ASSOCIATION
NATIONAL TENPOINT LEADERSHIP FOUNDATION
NGO COMMITTEE ON THE FAMILY Austria
ORGANIZATION TUNISIENNE DE L'EDUCATION ET
   DE LA FAMILLE (OTEF) Tunisia
PARENTAL STRESS LINE
PARENTING COALITION INTERNATIONAL
PARENTING EDUCATION NETWORK -- See
   NATIONAL PARENTING EDUCATION NETWORK
PARENTING EDUCATION NETWORK of
   Massachusetts
PARENTING EDUCATION & SUPPORT FORUM
   United Kingdom
The PARENTING JOURNEY
PARENTS ANONYMOUS
PARENTS, FAMILIES AND FRIENDS OF LESBIANS
   AND GAYS (PFLAG)
PARENTS FORUM
PARENTS HELPING PARENTS
PARENTS TELEVISION COUNCIL
PARENTS WITHOUT PARTNERS
PHARE Pour l'Harmonie des Relations Enfant-
   Parents France
PRODDER Programme for Development Research
   South Africa
PROJECT PARENTS
PTA -- See NATIONAL PTA
RESPECT FOR PARENTS DAY
ROTARY International
SAMARITANS / SAMARITEENS
SPAN/SUICIDE PREVENTION AWARENESS
   NETWORK
TOUGHLOVE® International
TUNISIAN ORGANIZATION FOR EDUCATION AND

THE FAMILY (OTEF) Tunisia
TV FREE AMERICA
UNITED NATIONS Family Unit
VIVA RIO Brazil
VOLUNTEER SOLUTIONS
WORLD LEARNING
YOUNG AUDIENCES

ACKNOWLEDGEMENTS

My gratitude list starts with my parents, Dick and Louise Odiorne, no longer living, whom I thank for their energy and inspiration. Also I am happy to have known all four of my grandparents, Kitty Grandmother and Grandfather George Harris, Grandfather Ralph and Grandmother Helen Odiorne. I cherish a childhood shared with my sister Corinne and my brother Ken. My friendships with them, with Corinne's husband Daniel and their girls, Helen and Rose, with Ken's wife Chris and their three children, Geoffrey, Maggie and Tommy, are also treasures to me. Of the several other-mothers and other-fathers and the many neighbors and coworkers who helped me along the way, Beverly and Read Viemeister, Florence O'Hare, and Herman Feshbach, deserve special mention. I have learned a great deal from each of them... how to be as well as what to do, in life.

Joe, my ex-husband, gave me the chance to be a mother, and I am grateful to him every day for Rich, Luke and Michael. Joe also suggested to Merid, one of his students from Ethiopia, that he ask me for a room in my house. That short-term, exchange student arrangement began in the late 80's when Merid was attending high school with Rich and Luke. Over

191

the years Merid has become a wonderful brother for our three. People ask if I adopted Merid. I didn't, but he adopted us. I appreciate Joe's family and Merid's family too for their many kindnesses. Thanks especially to the four of you boys, for your patience and love in raising me as a parent.

I have immense gratitude to PARENTS FORUM co-founder Christine Bates, founding board member Mary McCormack and early, long-time supporters Miriam Hadley, Karen Kosco and Angel Zamora. Deep thanks are due to other PARENTS FORUM board members and advisors, past and present, Alexander Belopolsky, Tim Cunningham, Mike Borruso, Nina Breygin, Bonny Carroll, Dan Dangler, Darlene Hawkins, Gene Kalaw, Emma Lathan, Arlene Lowney, Mary McPeak, Paul Nicholson, Marsha Orent, Margaret Serpa, Steven Stathis, Lois Sullivan, Natalie Thue, and Howard Wolfe. For patience and under-standing, thanks also to family members of these wonderful folks. Thanks as well to participants, vol-unteers, and sponsors for contributions of time, goods, services, and most of all your good energies.

Suzanne Wildman introduced me to Martha Mulligan who edited this book. I simply could not have written it without your help! Heartfelt thanks to you both and to Fletcher Moore, typesetter extra-ordinaire. Designers Marie Sherican and Jana Bull and illustrator Martina Marek merit special men-tion for their excellent professional work and for the handholding this first-time author needed.

Community members in Cambridge and Somerville who have encouraged and advised me at key points over the past years include John Altobello, MIT stu-dents Sean Barrett and Shirley Lai who co-wrote our first business plans for the MIT Entrepreneurs

Club 10K Competitions, Armando, Bill Bates, Ginny
Berkowitz and others involved with Cambridge
Community Television, Fred Berman, Beverly
Cassara, Charlie Christopher, Pat Dailey, Ann
Dausch, Adina Davidson, Vince Dixon, Francis
Duehay, Ariela and Uri Friedman, Sarah Fugiwara,
Margaret Gallagher and Cambridge Public School
Department parent liaisons, Sarah Gallop, Margaret
Ann Gray, Nancy Hoe and other members of the
Cambridge Family Literacy Coalition, Bret Henry,
Bob Hurlbut, Derrick and Michelle Jackson, Rick
Jarvis, Lee George Jefferson, Jean Jeune, Eileen
Keegan, Jack Langstaff and everyone at Revels,
Todd Marinoff, Daryl Mark and Susan Flannery and
Cambridge Public Library staff, Denise Maguire and
Cambridge Family and Children's Services staff,
Dave Massé, Monica Murphy, Joel Nitzberg, Judy
and Jack Palmer, Michelle Phelan, Gus Rancatore,
Margaret Rueter, Dorothy Scotten, Carolyn Shipley,
Richard Shyduroff, Doug Ling and others involved
with the MIT Entrepreneurs Club, Rae Simpson and
Kathy Simons at MIT Family Resource Center,
Walter Sullivan and Michael Sullivan, Karen Swaim,
Phoebe Wells and other home-schooling parents,
and Alice Wolf. The program has received help from
members of the Cambridge and Somerville
Chambers of Commerce, the Somerville Lions Club
and Somerville Kiwanis, the Rotary Clubs of
Cambridge, Brookline and several other Boston area
cities and towns, and political officials in both
Cambridge and Somerville. Also we have received
valuable pro bono professional services from local
attorneys and printing companies.

Folks from away who have helped our program in
various ways include Ruth Bhengu from South
Africa, Marilyn Dalrymple from Lancaster,
California, Luc and Nicole Dupont in Québec,

Amr Ghaleb in New York City, Sweet Alice Harris in Watts, Yoshie Kaga at UNESCO in Paris, Corinne Kumar from Tunis, Melody Mograss and Richard Giasson in Montreal, Dr. Ana Mon from Argentina, Sally Rogers in Connecticut, Belinda Rollins in Washington DC and Patty Wipfler from California. The folks at iComm in Toronto hosted our website for several years, as did MIT -- thank you, Suzana Lisanti. We also thank Pippin Petty-Schropel at CyberAccess who presently hosts our site. Members of the International Federation for Parent Education and staff and members of CIVICUS and ISTR (International Society for Third Sector Research) as well as volunteers and staff of World Boston have shared good thoughts with me on many occasions, in person and by email.

National Writers Union members have also encouraged me and the program has benefitted from contacts with Liane Hansen of National Public Radio, Alison Bass of the Boston Globe and several editors and writers at the Cambridge Chronicle, Somerville Journal and Somerville News.

Any gratitude list that left off friends and neighbors would be incomplete indeed. Teachers, parents, parent liaisons and after-school program staff at Fitzgerald, Agassiz, Cambridge Rindge and Latin Schools, teachers and parents at Cambridge Ellis School, and the sisters and teachers at North Cambridge Catholic High School have been wonderfully supportive as have teachers and fellow students from Bryan High School in my home town of Yellow Springs, Ohio. With apologies for any unintended omissions, thank you to Julie Loud Albertin, Len Alford, Stephen Allsop, Luzette and Dionisio Bazeia, Habib Ben Yahia, Pat Berkeley, Ellie Bonsaint, Kay and Steve Borgeson, Fatma and

Bechir Bouraoui, Catherine Brentani, Sarah Brill, Peter and Bea Britton, Michael Buss, Chuck and Rita Colbert, Kim and Kate DeRiel, Rae and George Dewey, Dick and Suanne Dillman, Joan Doucette, Pam and Bob Ellison, Jean Flanagan, Meron Getaschew, Cheryl and Brian Gillespie, Pumla Gobodo-Madikizela, Bill and Barbara Golder-Novick, Charlotte Gordon, Deb Gould, Jenny and Walter Gundy, Julie Hammond-Coiro, Sylvio and Blondine Hyppolite, Junko Izumi, George Jenkins, Kim Joy, Louise Kelliher, Carol and Chuck Koeller, Katya Kohn, Betsy Kostic, Cindy Lewis, Pat and Kevin Lowther, Elsye Luc, Sharon McBride, Barry and Jackie Megquire, Judy and John Moynihan, Ricky Murphy, Margaret and Jonathan Myers, the O'Hare Family, Ron Harris, Cristina Oliveira, Tjerk and Jannette Oosterkamp, Bob Petitti, Molly Porter, Teddy Primack, AnneMarie Regazoni, Ron and Christine Reilly, Nancy Rial, Gloria Rivers, Gil Sakakeeney, El Hadj Sarr, Rich and Sue Silva, the Slepecky family, Lee Smith, Emmi Snyder, Avi Soifer and Marleen Booth, Gillian Solomons, Charlie and Donna Souris, Marilou and John Spash, Barry Unger, Laura van Dam, Beverly Viemeister, Anil Vij, Chun Yi Wang, Sally Waters, David Whitmore, Essia Klila Zaouche, and Tita and Angel Zamora Sr., Jay and Yael Zif.

Also, the theoretical physics folks, Laboratory for Nuclear Science staff and Women's Forum colleagues at MIT are an inspiration. I love working with you all.

Besides all my agemates to thank -- and one nice thing about being (finally) "grown-up" is that age-mates can be anywhere from 35 to 75 -- there are my kids' friends, many of whom have become my friends too. They keep me up-to-date on current music and vocabulary and help me avoid a too-early senility.

Friends in the Deaf community, Jason Hurdich, Nancy Becker, Ruth Moore, Rita Straubhaar and Brenda Schurtz especially, and American Sign Language interpreters including Rebekkah Barkowitz, Celia Halstead, Tom Westcott and Jody Steiner opened my eyes to aspects of culture and communication that were entirely foreign to me.

Guests in my home over the last eighteen-plus years have, similarly, shared their experiences and taught me a great deal. Friends I've met at conferences in the US and elsewhere have opened their hearts and, sometimes, their homes to me! To those helpful people whose names I have forgotten, apologies. To everyone, especially those who prefer to remain anonymous, thank you, thank you, and thank you. Biases and mistakes that remain, I claim.

The anxieties that too often made me feel like a beggar fade away in the warmth of the friendship you have shown me. If wishes were horses, beggars would ride. Here I am, not riding, but writing. Even better!

AFTERWORD

Please participate in our next book by sending us your answers to any or all of the eight questions which can be found on page 60. Kindly include a brief description of yourself: age, gender, family situation (including ages of your children if you are a parent) and where you are from. Please include your name, unless you wish your contribution to be anonymous. Thank you!

ABOUT THE AUTHOR

Eve Sullivan founded PARENTS FORUM as a way to pass along the help she received from other parents during a family crisis. She trained to be a French teacher and presently works at the Massachusetts Institute of Technology as editorial assistant for a physics journal. Previously she taught English as a Second Language in Massachusetts as well as in Portugal and Tunisia. She has three grown sons and counts as part of her family a young man from Ethiopia.

ABOUT THE PROGRAM

PARENTS FORUM began in 1991 as a column in the bimonthly North Cambridge News (Cambridge, Mass. USA). The program was organized informally by Eve Sullivan and Christine Bates in October of that year and incorporated in 1992. The program received United States Internal Revenue Service determination of status as a 501(c)(3) non-profit organization in 1993. This determination was reaffirmed in 1999.

In 1993 the program was given a special "Social Venturing Award" as a socially responsible business idea by the Entrepreneurs Club of the Massachusetts Institute of Technology. In 1994 the Massachusetts Volunteer Network gave PARENTS FORUM an Honorable Mention as "Program of the Year."

Contact PARENTS FORUM
by postal mail:
144 Pemberton Street
Cambridge MA 02140-2509 USA
Tel: 617 - 864-3802
by email: info@parentsforum.org

and please visit us on the web:
www.parentsforum.org

COLOPHON

Editing
by Martha Hooper

Cover and book art direction
by Jana Bull

Design and illustrations
by Marie Sheridan

Additional illustrations
by Martina Marek

Typesetting
by Fletcher Moore, Salty Dog Design

Set in Bookman Old Style typeface
Printed by BookMasters on windsor vellum.

NOTES

906